NOT JUST A ONE NIGHT STAND

MINISTRY WITH THE HOMELESS

John Flowers and Karen Vannoy

DISCIPLESHIP RESOURCES

P O BOX 340003 • NASHVILLE, TN 37203-0003

www.discipleshipresources.org

ISBN 978-0-88177-557-0
Library of Congress Control Number 2009921841

Second Printing: 2010

CONTENTS

FOREWORD

The Christ who is Lord of the Church stands at the margins of the world. To forget either Christ as Lord or the Christ at the margins is to lose our way as the Church. As Lord Christ provides the story for our lives—the story that is to be the more encompassing story of all we are and do—our task is not to put the story of Christ in the world's story, but to place the world's story in that of Christ. This is to claim Christ as Lord.

At the same time, basic to the story of Christ is the one who comes to us in those who are least in our own eyes and in the eyes of the world. To see Christ as only high and lifted up, as exalted—in the world's terms—is to miss the character of the wisdom of God; it is to fail to understand the Christ who comes in the excluded, the exploited, the oppressed, and the people who "ain't right."

In this faith-inspiring book, John Flowers and Karen Vannoy call the church again to the Christ who is Lord who appears at the margins of established, respectable life. Their long co-pastorate at the Travis Park United Methodist Church in San

Antonio, Texas, is a moving testimony to what can happen in a church that makes Christ Lord and looks for that Lord on the margins. The work of that church and these two co-pastors with the homeless must certainly be one of the most effective and faithful witnesses in the United States in recent years.

I am struck by how much this ministry assumed that the work *with* the homeless had to be a work *of* the homeless. Constantly drawing on the perspectives of the marginal and the sagacity they possessed, the ministry of The Travis Park Church avoided many errors, but more important, moved compassionately because of its good sense to learn from the poor and to make use of their gifts and graces.

Flowers and Vannoy make it clear that this work is not a one night stand. It is a work that requires ongoing, hard, resource challenging, persistent effort that can learn from its mistakes and is not afraid to think outside the box. It is a ministry that will experience failure—sometimes tragic failure—but it is a ministry that calls the church into the very presence of Christ.

Churches considering or involved in homeless ministries will find here the kinds of teachings that are utterly crucial to such work. These pages provide ideas that are sometimes so very simple but not usually considered. It is the skills of a church that has learned from the poor and the homeless. We often forget that discipleship is a craft, one to be learned from those highly skilled in the trade. This book offers that kind of training where the homeless are the trade association and the church and its pastors are apprentices.

I am touched over and over again by the stories of the

homeless and the ministry of this church and its pastors. The preacher looking for the right story for a Sunday sermon will find many candidates in these pages. The humor, the pathos, the tragedy, the loss, the hope, and the uncanny moves in order to serve the homeless: all of these are found here in a moving narrative embodiment.

I have not mentioned the people you will meet here. Queen Margaret and the importance of community to her schizophrenic struggle; Julian, who hears voices; Luther, who dies a tragic death; the transfiguration of Adam; and many others. You will learn of how differently they read the Scriptures from the way the affluent middle class does.

Here we see the importance of eating with the homeless, listening to their stories, worshipping together, and learning to think indigenously. We confront the limits of charity and the problems of giving money to the poor. We receive instruction on the importance of birthday parties and picnics in the park as contemporary forms of the use of festival with the powerless to bring them into community and to move toward transformation.

But I mention only a few of the things to be learned and by which to be motivated to get out of our settled living and into a vital ministry with the poor and the homeless. I pray that you will be blessed by this book as I was, that it will leave you so uncomfortable with its passion and its hope that you, as I am, are moved to a ministry with the homeless that is not just a one night stand.

Tex Sample

PREFACE

Jesus said "the poor will always be with you," and we are both resentful and relieved at his words. On the one hand, we resent that he seems to accept what we know is a grinding dead end for too many lives. From him, we want vision for a new heaven and a new earth. On the other hand we are relieved because all of our efforts and prayers seem to accomplish so little. The government's war on poverty grinds on, while the churches continue to take up offerings. Social workers are overwhelmed, and compassion fatigue overtakes us in the face of so much suffering. We want to make a difference, but what can one person do? For that matter, what can one church do? Even Jesus seemed to believe poverty was inevitable, so we turn our attention to the places where our efforts produce results.

Then there's a knock on our door. Not a position paper on the subject of poverty, but a flesh and blood human being stands there, hoping we will answer. His name is Manuel, and his shirt is turned inside out. His voice barely audible, he is unable or unwilling to answer even half of the questions we ask. He doesn't have a current address, he has been on and off the streets for years. His mother lives in town, and he doesn't have a job. We ask if he is hungry. He says, "Yes." We give him some peanut butter, crackers, fruit juice and other non perishables. He leaves our front porch asking permission to sit down on the curb outside our home to eat the food we gave him. We say, "yes," peel back the curtain, and watch him carefully spread the peanut butter with the plastic knife. There is the fear of violence from strangers which chills our response; but there is also the fear of entanglement with a high maintenance man who lives in poverty.

As for Manuel, he eats this meal like most of his meals, sitting alone with no one to talk to. He's used to it now. It is rare that someone will even make eye contact with him, much less exchange greetings. Manuel may be struggling with an untreated mental illness, or losing a battle with addiction. Then again, he may be just plain dog tired and unable to reach a shelter by meal time. The scene repeats itself throughout the day, the week, and the country; no community is exempt. There is obviously something wrong, with him, with us, and with our whole social framework for dealing with poverty.

We did not write this book to call attention to Manuel's transformation and others who struggle as he struggled. We wrote this book because of the startling discovery we made when we finally had our eyes opened. We need to change. We need to do more than hand out food. We need to hear another's story. We need to partner with human beings moving forward.

We need to understand more about poverty and what is happening with persons on the margins. We need a whole new perspective. We wrote this book because of our corporate failure, and our deep faith in the capacity of our society, our churches, and our governments to make a difference.

Though the names have been changed, the stories are real. These are stories of church people who made a difference. These are stories of dignity, respect, and transformation. It is our hope that you might see another way to connect across socio-economic lines with persons who are poor. It is our hope that you will build community with someone who wants to share a meal with you whether it's under a bridge, on the street, or inside your church.

We would like to thank Glide Church in San Francisco for mothering us to this deeper vision, and the people of Travis Park UMC in San Antonio for traveling with us on this journey. We thank Tex Sample for his consistent encouragement as we composed the words for these pages. We would also like to thank Discipleship Resources for agreeing to partner with us to get this message out to you.

John and Karen

CHAPER 1

OUR HEARTS ARE IN THE RIGHT PLACE

Local churches help people in need. Whenever there is human suffering, the church is sure to appear with a helping hand. As the church, we come with the best of intentions. Our hearts are in the right place. The problem comes when we take our heartfelt concerns and put them into action. Usually we never stop to evaluate our work and look at the results our programs are having. If we do, we find our charity fails to produce what we intended. We had hoped for suffering to ease and new lives to begin. We had hoped we would be able to do what Jesus asked us to do: When you see someone thirsty, give him drink; if naked, provide clothing and when hungry, feed them. So we set about the task, then the next day, there the same individuals are again: thirsty, naked, and hungry. Are these the results we want? Is this really what Jesus meant?

All over America, downtown churches are increasingly overwhelmed with requests from poor and marginalized people in desperate need. The churches band together under the assumption that as a group we can do far more than any one local church could do on its own and form a coalition to provide ministry and assistance to those in need. In some cities, this effort expands beyond food pantries and clothes closets into classes on household budgeting and assistance with rent or utilities. At first, there are lots of volunteers and plenty of resources, but over time both get scarce, in part due to the success of the work itself. Demand catches up with supply and forces limitations on the assistance given. Suggestions turn into experimentation which turns into guidelines which ultimately become the new rules. The number of visits per person to the clothes closet is limited to once a week, as is the amount of clothing which can be given out. Similar rules are made for groceries. Financial assistance for utilities and rent becomes limited to $100.00 once a quarter, regardless of how much is actually needed.

What is initially an attempt by good-hearted people to introduce a standard of fairness becomes a hard and fast rule to be enforced. Volunteers are drawn into policing the policy and enforcing the rules. Some persons are turned away hungry or with clothes in tatters because they fail to fit into the new rules. It becomes harder and harder to get new volunteers to serve inside such a system, so operating hours are reduced. City Assistance Ministry, once extending hours into the evening, now is open 9:00 AM to 4:00 PM. The working poor, those trying to survive on hourly wage jobs, are unable to get to the facility during those operating hours, but the numbers are made up by those who live entirely off the welfare system.

With fewer volunteers comes more difficulty in sustaining funding from individual contributing congregations. The city and county governments begin to step in to provide financial support from grants and other forms of subsidy. However, their support comes with strings attached: numbers and paperwork. The more people the ministry serves, the more money the ministry can receive from grants. Rent and utility subsidy become limited to $75.00 every other month so more persons can be served. Clothes closet visits are restricted to once a month. Groceries are given only to those with kitchens. More people are served, but fewer needs are being met.

At one point a policy decision is made to limit financial assistance again. The dollar amount of the monies received from the city will be divided by the number of persons assisted the previous year. If this comes to $280 per person, then clients can request financial assistance for utilities, rent subsidy, etc., on a quarterly basis, and receive up to $70 with each request. As this rarely amounts to the total actually needed, clients are encouraged to contact churches directly who have discretionary monies. Churches once again are invited to become social workers trying to evaluate need and wind up establishing a set amount to be given, saying "This is all we can give this time."

The poor go from church to church, trying to piece together the $185.00 necessary to actually prevent the utilities from being disconnected. No real effort is made anywhere to tie the assistance to any kind of long term recovery. Occasionally, courses are offered in financial management, but if you don't have money, the information drops into a vacuum and is of little help. The next quarter the whole process is repeated.

This puts the poor person in the difficult position of never being able to be free from outside assistance; the cycle of poverty cannot be broken. On the other hand, this allows the church coalition group to increase by five times the recorded number of people helped, which results in increases in funding the next year. Consequently, the churches feel good about what is being done, and the coalition ministry becomes the city's bulwark against poverty. In reality, the ministry has become part of the cycle.

Meanwhile, poor families continue to be buried in bills with little hope for the future. It may sound fair, but in reality, life doesn't work that way. With a $70 payment, the utility company won't leave the lights on if you owe them $350 after months of non-payment. Neither will a landlord look the other way if provided one fifth of a month's rent, especially if you only paid half the rent last month. In fairness, they aren't equipped to be in the subsidy business. While our agencies look good on paper because they "help" so many people, it takes more than a partial payment to keep the lights on and a roof over your head. So eventually the poor family winds up homeless.

Homelessness creates other social problems which are of great concern to most Christians. Throughout the country, churches band together to provide shelter and new ministries are formed. The story for the shelters is much the same everywhere, born out of real human suffering.

During an unseasonably cold winter night in south Texas, a pastor of a prominent church in the downtown area was approached by a man who was obviously poor. He needed food. He needed a place to sleep. This pastor had a heart for the poor. He gave the man what little money he carried in his wallet. This was enough for food but not shelter for the night. The panhandler was grateful for the meal money but it was late, dark, and growing cold and this was a night where few could sleep on the streets and stay warm.

The picture of this man, trying to make the best of his situation, haunted the pastor on his way home. He said a prayer and asked God to watch over the one who had no place to lay his head. "It is biblical," he said to himself, "foxes have dens, birds have nests, but the son of man has no place to lay his head . . . ."

In the morning, there was evidence that the wanderer had tried to create a makeshift sleeping area behind the shrubbery, close to the office, using the walls as a guard against the wind. The pastor recognized his visitor from the night before, went over to let him know it was time to move on, but the man did not move. He had died sometime during the night. Filled with outrage from the tragedy and vowing to make sure this never happened again, this pastor became the organizing force behind a shelter to house persons who are, for whatever reason, homeless for the night.

Similar stories lie behind shelters in most major cities, with other churches joining the effort with money and volunteer help. The need is so great and the task so complex, that local governments get involved, providing some operational funding and often rent-free facilities. What all these communities have in common is the desire to provide safe place for homeless persons to sleep. Their hearts are in the right place. What the administrators and volunteers at the shelter want is to help people less fortunate than themselves. Their hearts are in the right place, too, but providing an alternative to sleeping under the stars is a social problem with no perfect solutions

What starts out as compassion and the desire to provide protection and dignity soon becomes the task of simply maintaining order. Here are some rules for a typical 300 bed facility:

- Doors open at 4:00 PM and close at 5:00 PM or until all beds are full
- Metal detectors are at the door
- Backpacks and belongings are not allowed in the sleeping quarters
- Breathalyzers are at the door and no one is allowed entry if their blood alcohol level is over the legal limit
- Everyone must leave at 6:00 AM, no exceptions
- Families may not stay together; all are segregated by gender

One friend who lives on the street and clearly struggles with his untreated mental illness, describes his overnight stay at a local shelter.

"You are afraid to close your eyes and go to sleep. All the bunks are pushed close together. I look to the guy on my right and he wants to steal my stuff. I look to the one on my left and he beat me up the week before. I would rather take my chances on the street. The volunteers there are good-hearted people, but they can't do anything after the lights go out."

But in the church we feel better knowing there's a place for them to go. No one needs to freeze to death ever again.

All the problems faced by the middle class in our communities are also faced by the poor and marginalized, including the healthcare crisis. In any metropolitan area today, you will find healthcare clinics for the poor and marginalized people. Most of the clinics started out small, with one clinic and one doctor whose heart was in the right place, usually donating the time. One clinic becomes two, two becomes four, and four becomes eight. The need is great and these clinics relieve the pressure on local emergency rooms, that without these clinics, would often see patients whose presenting complaints are far from life threatening. The underserved, uninsured poor gained access to healthcare in the form of a visit to the doctor's office.

One clinic was established inside a local shelter. The logic was to bring a clinic operation to the desperately poor at a site where poor and marginalized people congregate. Hard working, underpaid doctors, nurses, and healthcare professionals staffed the clinic. It was a surprise to learn that the biggest struggle in this endeavor was to convince the population to use their services.

At the same time, another modest clinic effort was growing in a downtown church each Sunday morning. Volunteer
doctors, nurses, and church members staffed that clinic; the
working poor as well as homeless persons came in overwhelming numbers every Sunday morning, and soon the word
spread. Many of the patients who came to the modest church
clinic stayed overnight at the shelter but would not come to
the shelter's medical clinic, even though the shelter's clinic had
superior access to pharmaceuticals and follow-up medical care.
Leaders from the public medical clinic in the shelter came to
the church clinic, genuinely perplexed because homeless persons would not come to them for healthcare services, but
would instead walk down the street to the church's clinic.
They asked the church, "Why will the people choose to come
here when we have a greater capacity to serve their need at our
location?"

"We don't know," we answered. "Let's go ask them."
Taking a microphone that next Sunday morning, in front of
125 persons who had settled in for their complimentary breakfast, we asked, "Why do you patronize our church clinic when
there is an excellent clinic at the shelter that goes largely
unused?" One after one the answers poured in.

"This clinic takes walk-ins. We have to make an appointment
at the county clinic."

"This clinic does not have a lot of rules. The county clinic has
rules."

"The church clinic doesn't have a bunch of forms to fill out
like that other place."

"Here we don't have to take a number."

"At the county clinic we wait forever, and we get prescriptions for medicines, then we have to apply for help to pay for the medicines, then we have to wait for approval, and then have to go across town to pick up the medicine."

But the answer which received the most nods of agreement was

"Here, at the church clinic, we are treated with *dignity and respect.*"

We reported the results of this informal survey to those who asked the question. The leaders of their clinic operation asked if we would be open to receiving their expertise inside our clinic.

"Absolutely! But you must understand that we do not use a medical delivery model, we use a holistic medicine model. We believe that a medical clinic visit is about more than treating and diagnosing from a presenting complaint. It's about caring as much about the person's spirit as their physical health. It's about doctors and nurses letting patients know that they, too, are as frail and vulnerable as the patient is. The church's clinic is about addressing the spiritual needs which weave through all our lives and every illness. We believe in learning from each other. We understand that poverty has a spiritual component, which we try to address. We need our clinic healthcare professionals to be comfortable with these pre-suppositions as well."

The conversation did not die, and yet the differences in philosophy and style were too much to overcome. We did develop a workable partnership with the county clinics that resulted in patient referral for more specialized concerns and long-term treatment. Maybe sometimes people with their hearts in the right place grow their relief efforts too fast and too far beyond where they can comfortably show the love they want to show. When there are hundreds of people per day who need help, but only a handful of good-hearted people available for four hours per day to administer that help, the volunteers will be overwhelmed and burnout will inevitably follow.

The little church clinic operated for only two hours on Sunday morning. Even with three doctors and two nurses in attendance, the maximum number of people seen in those two hours was 30. No doctor can see more than five patients per hour and treat them all with dignity and respect. There is constant pressure to expand a helping program into a service delivery model, or to move past calling people by name into assigning persons a number. But there are plenty of clinics that operate that way; the church was offering something different.

Sometimes our hearts are in the right place, but that's not enough. We have to enssure the action we take is the action that is needed. Sometimes the voice of the church will be the only voice on the side of the poor.

One Texas city was rated as #17 one year on the national list for meanest American cities in the treatment of persons who happen to be homeless. The city had risen to these heights when the local city government passed four quality of life municipal ordinances against unwanted behavior.

- no one is allowed to block a public sidewalk and prevent another from passing
- no camping out in public places
- no panhandling
- no urinating or defecating in public
- Any violation of any above stated ordinance receives a citation and is subject to a fine of up to $500 dollars.

Everyone should have free passage on public streets. No one can quarrel with that. In our observation of persons who happen to be poor, we found that allowing panhandling or begging contributes to the problem of poverty. (More on this later)

The ordinance about "camping out" in public places is a euphemism for sleeping in a public place. This may seem reasonable until you consider how many people have nowhere else to sleep but in a public place. If you have no home, and the shelters are full, exactly what are you supposed to do? Not sleeping is simply not an option for the human body. At some point your humanness takes over, and the body will fall asleep whether in public or private. We can make all the laws we want, but the laws will have no effect on the human body's inability to go without sleep, and the social problem that some persons have no place to sleep but in public.

The situation is similar with the ordinance against urinating or defecating in public. On the surface this seems not only fair, but a necessary health prohibition. However, if you have *no place* to eliminate bodily waste, (and this is true of all homeless people from time to time), exactly what are your options?

At the time when these ordinances were passed there were no public restrooms available in the "meanest" city between the hours of 11:00 PM and 7:00 AM, and generally no open restrooms on Saturday or Sunday. Some nightclubs would charge the homeless brothers and sisters $1 to come into their club and use the restroom. If a person didn't have a dollar and it was after 11:00 PM at night, then there was no other option for them than to relieve themselves in an alleyway or parking lot.

One Saturday evening as a pastor left the building, Luther, a homeless man who worshiped with us each Sunday, approached and asked to use the bathroom. He was drunk and she was late getting home, and she told him no. He cried as urine began to run down his leg, wetting his blue jeans through. There was nowhere for him to go. No business would let him in, and no public restrooms were open. The plight of the pastor worried about her safety is understandable; the plight of the brother who happened to be homeless was heart-rending.

Isn't it a justice issue to ban public human behavior, which is normal and necessary to survival, a crime when the person has no alternative? We are asking someone to choose to not fall asleep or not urinate when we all recognize that at some point, no human being can choose to avoid either behavior. At that point, we're punishing them when they do in public that which eventually the body cannot stop.

If a person falls asleep somewhere, and that person has no money for a motel and cannot gain entry to a shelter, they have no option but to sleep outside. On any given night in San Antonio there are 1,200 persons who happen to be homeless and only 300 beds available for overnight shelter. That is 900 persons each night without a bed indoors. They have no other option than to violate the ordinance. The 300 beds are available if, and only if, the person can pass a breathalyzer test.

Most shelters open their doors at 4:00 PM. Researchers conclude that one third of our chronic homeless population suffers from alcohol abuse. An untreated alcoholic taking a drink after 12:00 noon on any given day will not be able to pass a breathalyzer test at 4:00 PM that same day. The only option for the one who is homeless and suffers from the disease of alcoholism is to sleep outdoors.

The American Medical Association recognizes that alcoholism is a disease; therefore, we are criminalizing the behavior of someone who suffers from this disease and does not have a home. One third of any homeless population also suffers from untreated mental illness. Many of those who struggle with mental illness without proper treatment self-medicate with alcohol so there is a lot of overlap here. Someone who suffers from untreated paranoid schizophrenia will not sleep in a shelter due to their disease. Their delusions collide with the tight, closed quarters and lack of privacy, and they can spiral out of control. Therefore, sleeping indoors at a shelter is not a viable option for upwards to two-thirds of persons who happen to be homeless on any given night.

The heart of the community was in the right place, and there was a gathering to give voice to that heart. A "Hold It" campaign was held in a local park where the homeless congregated. Persons were encouraged to come from all over to the central city park and protest the injustice of the "no urinating or defecating in public" ordinance. People were encouraged to take one night and "hold it." Try to refrain from using the restroom between the hours of 11:00 PM and 7:00 AM just one night.

Any man over 50 years of age knows the impossibility of the task! From the heart, and with the voice of the people, came action from the city. In short order, four different downtown 24/7 access restrooms were in the planning and construction process. People are compassionate: they will not tolerate injustice when they understand the human story of suffering.

We have friends who know poverty up-close and personal. Their names are Luther, Robert, Gloria, Wanda, Alan, Detroit, Sam, Isaiah, and Frank. We haven't begun to name them all but you get the picture. These are people we came to know through ministry in downtown San Antonio. We were pastors of a downtown church in a unique ministry with the poor and marginalized (that is *with*, not *to*, the poor and marginalized people). We gradually were faced with an uncomfortable realization: few of us really know what it feels like to be desperately poor, yet we study poverty and call ourselves experts.

An announcement about a church-sponsored continuing education event in a nearby town was placed entitled "Ministry with the Poor and Marginalized." Here was a great opportunity for our friends, who had taught us a lot, to teach others and make more friends. We called the one who was identified as the contact person for this session. The conversation went something like this:

"I see you are having a session on Ministry with the Poor and Marginalized and we would like to bring some persons who know poverty first-hand to be a part of your seminar."

"Yes," she responded, "We would love to have your group attend our session, be sure to register soon because we have limited enrollment."

"To be honest, I had hoped that these persons who knew poverty and marginalization first-hand could participate as session leaders for the class."

"I'm sorry, I will be the leader."

"Perhaps the folks who come with us could assist you in the teaching?" I questioned.

"I don't think I can do that."

"I'm sorry, I'm afraid I don't understand"

"Have any of them been through our denomination's training?"

"Excuse me?"

"Teachers for this session have gone through extensive training at denominational headquarters. Have any of your friends been through the training?"

"No, they can't afford to attend the training. They are poor. Do you know any persons who are poor?"

"I'm sorry," she explained, "only leaders who have received the training are qualified to teach."

So it is that educated, urban, sophisticated middle- and upper-class folks continue to teach other educated, urban, sophisticated people about ministry with the poor and marginalized.

It is the same in the secular world. Quite by accident, we ran into a downtown businessman who was a supporter of our ministry. He asked us, "Are you going to the Downtown Chamber of Commerce's breakfast next week?" Once we explained we were not members of the chamber he told us more.

"Since you now are involved in ministry with poor and marginalized persons I thought you would be there because the program is entitled "The Homeless Problem" and you have friends who are homeless.

"Who is going to speak?" I asked

"Someone from the police bike patrol, the head of the homeless shelter, the city Council person from district one, and a representative of downtown businesses."

We found out the breakfast was to take place at an exclusive, member's only dining club in the center of the city, and we had an idea about expanding their program. At the next Wednesday night gathering of our prayer picnic, with the great majority of participants currently using the stars for their roof at night, John stood up near the conclusion and asked this question;

"How many of you have ever had breakfast at the Plaza club?" Not one hand was raised, so he continued.

"How many of you would attend this breakfast with me next Wednesday morning? My treat!" Twenty hands went up.

"My only rule is I won't buy your breakfast if you show up drunk." Promises were made all around.

John called the next day to make the reservations.

"I would like to reserve 15 places for the chamber breakfast next Wednesday where the presentation is on the homeless problem."

"Very well sir, are you a member?"

"No I am not."

"May I ask what company are you with?"

"I am with . . . (and named the church)"

"And your guests? Can I have the names of those who will be in attendance?"

Since John didn't know who would show up that morning because our friends from the street don't generally set their alarm clocks, and wake-up calls come at the end of a police officer's night stick, he said, "I don't have the names right now; can we fill out name tags when we arrive?"

"Of course, sir!" She was thrilled that they would have a big crowd next Wednesday and excited about the prospect of 15 potential members for the Chamber. We wondered how thrilled she would actually be when we showed up. We paid in advance with credit card information lest we be denied access at the door. Karen called a friend from the local paper and asked if she wanted to come along, and the reporter thought it would be great fun.

We arrived early the next Wednesday morning at the elevators on the ground floor of the bank building—12 homeless men and women and three of us who have roofs over our heads. The security guard was hesitant but cooperative when we explained our purpose and verified our reservations. We entered the Plaza club and caused quite a stir, and to their credit, the officers of the downtown Chamber were cordial and polite.

People were asked to get their food and then find a place to sit and eat. John was near the end of the line and was not surprised, once he had filled his plate, to find our homeless friends eating by themselves. It was easy to detect side glances from all around the room. We sat down with our friends and listened to the program. Most of the homeless folks were respectful of the speakers while going back for seconds and thirds. In due time, since our presence was too difficult to ignore, one of the social service agency presenters looked in our direction and said "We didn't know the pastors from the downtown church would be here. Perhaps you would come forward and share some thoughts on the homeless problem."

"With your permission, I would like to invite my friend Luther, who has been homeless for some time, to speak to us," John said. The look of discomfort on their faces was obvious, but they graciously agreed. Luther stood up and spoke eloquently about the need for public toilets, water fountains, and access to reading material to counteract the mind-numbing boredom and feelings of worthlessness carried by all who call the streets their home. Luther himself came close to tears explaining how sometimes he had needed to use the restroom so bad and no one would allow him access.

He explained what happens to the body when you need to urinate for hours and no one will allow it: "Eventually the urine just comes out, running down your leg and soaking your pants. Then, because you are homeless on a Saturday afternoon, with no other clothes available, you are left to spend the night in your wet pants. It's worse when it's cold, because they take so long to dry." As Karen remembered that Saturday afternoon at the church, the crowd listened in stunned silence. It was our first step in building support for making the changes the city needed to make.

Luther made friends that day teaching middle and upper class folks—politicians, public servants, and business men and women—how it feels to spend a day on the street. It was through friendships with Luther, Isaiah, Lady Margaret, Robert, John, Sam, Alan, and others that homelessness became personal to them.

Homelessness and poverty are not just issues for us any longer; now they have faces. Flesh and blood human beings suffer in desperate poverty. Temporary relief with a meal from a soup kitchen has no staying power. Partial utility subsidies look good on our agency records but do not help folks achieve stabilization.

For the most vulnerable of our brothers and sisters, one bed for one night, even in the most safe and secure surroundings, does not move people along their pathway of transformation. Empowering people for escape from desperate poverty is *not just a one night stand*. We need continuous, hands-on efforts that build community and sustain relationships across socio-economic lines. We need local churches involved in transformation. We can no longer be satisfied with one-way prayers to God, hoping for an outside miracle to eliminate grinding poverty. As Cecil Williams, pastor emeritus of Glide Memorial United Methodist Church in San Francisco once said, "I asked God every day to do something about the suffering of the homeless. Finally God said, 'Do it yourself!'"

CHAPTER 2

IS THIS YOUR CONGREGATION?

We Give Money

Volunteer Firefighters do it to buy equipment or simply to fund their operating budget for that year. Shriners do it to support their charity hospitals that serve children. Band and drill team members do it to march in far away parades. Standing on street corners, volunteer firefighters will use their boots as collection plates. The Shriners wear funny hats, sometimes dress as clowns riding go carts, and produce a well-marked container at the driver side window for contributions. A high school marching band or drill team will hold out a sign that proclaims "Rose Bowl Parade or Bust," and people roll down their windows and generously contribute, admiring the energy of youth. We will give to causes that we deem worthy. Some folks would even say "it is the Christian thing to do." Vying for busy intersections these days are poor persons, dressed in tattered and soiled clothes, holding up a crudely written cardboard sign with a message asking for help. Some examples are:

"Will Work for Food"

"Disabled Vet. Need Help"

"Out of work, hungry, need money"

"Tired, trying to get home. Any help appreciated, God bless"

"Babies hungry, need milk money. God bless"

Often times, accompanying the parent that holds this last sign is a toddler who plays quietly at her parent's feet. It tugs at the heart and so we give money, which eases our middle-class guilt, even though we know it doesn't change a life. We learned from those who live deep inside the world of poverty, that cardboard sign carriers are nearly always working a scam. Giving money not only produces a false sense of satisfaction; it perpetuates the system, keeping the poor dependent on the handout. Nearly every person on a street corner holding a cardboard sign is a con artist. These are smart people who have highly developed survival skills. Cardboard sign carrying panhandlers are usually creative and often ingenious in the ways they are able to tap into our middle class guilt and separate us from $1, $5, or even $10. It is best, however, if we refuse to give panhandlers money. The folks on the street will tell us that no matter how desperate the picture out the driver side window (some use small children in soiled clothes as props), don't give money. It is sad but true that a skilled, sign carrying, panhandler will earn more begging than they will in most entry level jobs. In her book *Nickel and Dimed: On (Not)*

Getting By in America, Barbara Ehrenreich demonstrates how difficult it is to survive on minimum wage jobs, a fact that persons mired in poverty have known for some time.

Driving into our city's airport we saw one friend at a busy intersection and he was hustling hard with his cardboard sign, "unemployed and hungry." As he approached the car and recognized us, his excuse poured out "I know how you hate this stuff and I'm not going to be here long. I just need 20 bucks and then I will stop, I promise. Two or three hours tops, and then I'm gone." Passing by that same intersection after we picked up our friend from the airport, he was gone. Sure enough, he had made his $20 and moved on. All intersections are not created equal. There are the premier spots for panhandling and then the lesser spots. The success of the professional beggars (and most of the cardboard sign intersection beggars we see *are* professionals), depends not only on creative writing skills, body language, and humble countenance, but also location. The coveted locations are staked out, and newcomers are trespassers and will be run off. The strong on the street always stake out the best claims.

Since most of us have hearts in the right place but lack the street smarts to discern legitimate need from the story of a con artist, many local churches create a "pastor's discretionary fund." We give money to ecumenical groups who serve the poor and hope this will keep the poor at bay. For those poor who show up at our doorstep, we rely on the pastor or church professional to hear the hard luck story, make a call on truth and voracity, and allocate funds to answer the need. In reality, few pastors have the street wisdom to pull this off. Courses in street smarts are not offered in our seminaries, and yet pastors in ministry with the poor and marginalized cannot survive without such an education. There are moments when persons at the church's doorstep are so scary, or their story is told in a way that is immune to independent verification, that we give money to them in hopes that they will go away. We (the authors) understand; we did it ourselves. The word out on the street is a church that gives money is either compassionate or an easy mark. Which description fits depends on the audience.

In an effort to do more than give money, we might have more conversations like this when confronted with emergency need:

"My mother is sick and dying in a Houston Hospital."

"I'm so sorry, I lost my mother years ago. I know that must be tough."

"Would you please buy me a bus ticket? I need to be with her and the bus leaves in one half hour."

"I'm really sorry, we don't do money. We used to do money and you're not going to believe this, but 90% of the folks who came through these doors with a sad story were just trying to con us. I don't question that your story is true and I hate it that those who came before you ruined it for everybody. I have been given clear instructions, though, and we can't do money."

"I'm not asking for money, just a bus ticket"

"I hear you, but it takes money to buy a bus ticket and we don't do money. We do food, clothing, medical care, dental and vision care, AA meetings, Bible study, and even work. You can earn money for that ticket through working here. Our work program begins on Monday. Come and sign up, and you might earn some money to buy that ticket."

"But she is expecting me there tonight!"

"I understand, and we can get you to Houston if you work with us."

"You obviously don't care!"

"Of course I care, but you came in here with a problem and said 'solve this problem my way.' I will help you solve the problem, but only if I can have a voice in what plan we use."

This takes more time than just giving out money, but giving money alone is not enough.

We Do "Drive By Charity"

It was just before Thanksgiving and the biggest hearted church members met in the fellowship hall to pick up their assignments. Each brown bag was filled with fixings for the upcoming holiday meal. Every volunteer picked up three or four bags, loaded them into the car and headed for the poor side of town. It was time for some "drive by charity." Volunteers arrived in a neighborhood mired in poverty, took one bag out, and carried this holiday meal to the nearest doorstep. After ringing the doorbell a silent prayer was lifted up by the delivery volunteer from the local church:

"Dear God, please let your light shine on me today and be gracious unto me. I pray that no one is home. Please allow me to drop this bag containing a holiday meal on this doorstep without anyone coming to the door lest I be caught in a protracted conversation and delayed from the remainder of my evening's business."

His prayers were answered; no one showed up at any one of homes where this volunteer made his delivery. The doxology was sung, the "less fortunate" were served, and the giver returns home feeling generous and compassionate, while the recipient family eats alone, wondering why dignity and respect are harder to find than a holiday meal.

We do "drive by charity." We do mission work in the ghettos and return to our gated neighborhoods. We tutor in underprivileged schools but won't let our own children attend there. Seventh Street was in the middle of a rough neighborhood. The street was full of crack houses and desperately poor, single-parent households. One church with significant resources went to 7th Street, set up a staging area for a Christian band, and began making music. Lawn chairs were set up. A crowd gathered, the music continued. Hot dogs were grilled and served to the neighborhood, adults, and children alike. The music played until about 3:00 PM then shut down, then band packed up the trailer. Cooks stowed their gear and grills. All the middle-class folks went home filled with the satisfaction that they had been the hands and feet of Jesus Christ that day, even though no relationships were nurtured and nothing changed. Most mission work shares one thing in common: We can leave, so we stay in our positions of protection and power.

We have been on many mission trips, and led one down to a small town in Mexico. It was a trip to deliver dental- and healthcare to the small mission church of that area, and we included a construction project where volunteers put a com position roof on the newly constructed chapel. On arrival to the site we found a palm tree growing in the middle of the nearly complete, four cinder block walls of the one room church.

"How silly they never cut down that tree at the beginning of construction," John thought. "Let's correct that mistake before we finish the walls." Convinced we arrived not a moment too soon to save these backward, small town, Mexican church folks from their ignorance of accepted construction practice, down came the tree, then up on the walls we climbed to do this the right way. As John worked with others on the wall at about 2:00 in the afternoon, he nearly had heatstroke. At the time the temperature climbed to its most unbearable height, he prayed for shade. Looking up towards the sun, John realized that had we not cut down that tree, we would have been covered in shade at that very moment. We had come to help, when in fact *we* were the one who needed new eyes and a better understanding.

During the daylight hours we lived and worked close to our Mexican neighbors. We ate our noon meal inside the dirt floor homes of the parishioners there. We ate chicken soup served from a pot in which you could see, should you care to look, the chicken's claw. Karen did intake at the medical clinic asking, "Que es dolor para usted?" (Where is your pain?). We traveled down unpaved dirt roads and worked cement without a cement mixer.

The people of this small town could not have accomplished what we did in those five days because we brought the resources, lumber, tar paper, shingles, and nails as well as cash to spread around local construction supply stores in ways this town had rarely seen. Then we went home to the U.S. and back into our protected, gated communities. Since we continued to serve that church another two years, we could see the degree of change that happened in most of the mission trip workers, and an observer would be hard pressed to see much different in their everyday lives.

Mission trips, whether they take us overseas or across town, affect us in a deep way. No one can judge the degree of inward transformation that takes place as a result of mission work, but Christianity calls us to more than an inward transformation; we are called to a transformation of our whole lives—not just how we think, but how we live. If it is just one week out of fifty-two, what are we accomplishing with our work? The poor are still impoverished, yet we have relieved our acute feelings of guilt. Most mission work shares one thing in common: we can leave and the recipients of our charity cannot.

We Send the Wrong Messages

Charity has become an ugly word because it usually defines a relationship where power is not shared. The messages in our conventional charity work are consistent and demeaning.

"We have a great deal and you have very little"

"We are not as broken as you are and we have come to help you."

"We feel sorry for you."

"We have made something of ourselves and you have not."

"We want to help you but we want you to be grateful."

Do the receivers of charity project these attitudes onto others, or do the volunteers in mission actually have these attitudes? We have found it to be a mixture of both, and the distance between us exacerbates the problem. These are the messages that make true community impossible. We are called to ministry *with* the poor as if they were Jesus himself, and we cannot do so with such messages.

In the urban church where I was a pastor, we served breakfast at no cost to all who showed up on Sunday morning. We soon discovered how hard it is to serve one plate after another while receiving mostly silence, grunts, or complaints about the food. At the end of a particularly exhausting morning in our first year of the Café, one volunteer asked, "Doesn't anyone say 'thank you' anymore?" Born out of frustration, this question reveals what many of us, whose hearts are in the right place, feel. We are motivated to serve because we are compassionate and we want to be liked.

We want to be congratulated for our generosity. We want to be appreciated. We want to be recognized for our selfless acts of human kindness. When people who happen to be poor do not respond as we expect, then we are quick to ask, "What is wrong with them?" If we step into the margins with folks who have lived there 24/7, the reasons become clear. Religious groups have a history of exacting a big price for a free breakfast. Some are willing to "pay the price" for their meal. "It may be free, but it ain't free!" one brother from the streets proclaimed.

I am all for saying grace and thanking God for the food before us, but many churches insist that their guests sit quietly through a Bible study before eating. "Fill the stomach and save the soul!" proclaimed a street preacher whose heart was in the right place. We might as well say at the beginning of these Bible studies, "We have not made a mess of our lives, you have. If you listen to us, then in return we will feed you." This is a demeaning message. We need to remind ourselves that Jesus never said, "Put the food away until the hungry can come with an appropriate attitude of gratitude." Jesus said feed the hungry, clothe the naked, visit the imprisoned, and welcome the stranger.

It was rare that anyone eating breakfast at the church on Sunday morning said, "thank you," or, "what a wonderful thing you are doing." This was hard on the volunteers and made them question their abilities to continue. Yet standing in a food line is what the poor do three times a day, seven days a week. It may be that we only work in the ministry once a week or less, so it's a big deal for us to be in this ministry. But the poor receive our handouts day in and day out. To most of them, it is no big deal because it's how they get by every single day. Our handout is what we have conditioned them to expect.

I mentioned before that our medical clinic was a modest operation for a couple of hours on Sunday morning. In the beginning, when the church started serving breakfast at no cost to all who were hungry, a physician friend and church member asked me if he could set up a table near the dining area and talk with individuals about their healthcare. He found a corner, commandeered a folding table, draped a stethoscope around his neck, and people came to talk with him about anything and everything, including their health.

Within a couple of years my friend was joined by other medical professionals, along with four exam rooms and a makeshift pharmacy. Still he struggled. One evening after dinner together in our home, he spoke of leaving our clinic work. He was discouraged. He talked of his frustrations with the guests. Some wouldn't take their medications, some continued to aggravate their already chronic conditions by continuing in self destructive behavior, and still others treated him with disrespect.

"I don't expect a lot, but no one appears to be appreciative and rarely do we receive a word of thanks from those who come to the clinic."

We had one of those relationships where we could speak honestly and openly with each other so I did not hold back. "Are you doing this to receive adulation or a 'thank you' from the guests? Do it instead for this one simple reason—because Jesus told you to do it!"

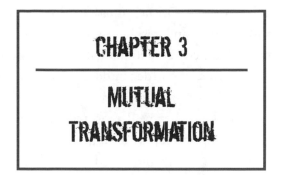

CHAPTER 3

MUTUAL TRANSFORMATION

The goal of our ministry in San Antonio became mutual transformation, and we work toward it through four pathways. The first two are for those who struggle with homelessness, chemical abuse, or untreated mental illness. The third pathway is directed at the adults and families who have slipped into homelessness when they fall on hard times. The fourth pathway is for us, you and me, respectable members of the middle and upper classes.

Untreated Mental Illness

Lady Margaret Worthington Ford was a frequent visitor to breakfast on Sunday mornings. Lady Margaret, sometimes calling herself queen Margaret, was untreated in her mental illness. She would eat breakfast alone, in the church's large fellowship hall. That was the way she wanted it. From her years of smoking, her voice was full of gravel and from her repetitive delusions, she had built a world that seemed to make sense to her, if not to others. On her most lucid days, she treated everyone with dignity and respect and insisted on the same from others. She was coy and coquettish with her physician at our clinic, her pastors, and other middle aged men in the congregation.

A doctor who knew her well reported she came to clinic for the intelligent conversation as much as for any medical care. Lady Margaret began most of her days with the same routine: as usual she has put on her make up and chosen her outfit with flair—this time jeans, grey sweater, black ankle-high shoes. Slouchy white hat, poofy blue boa, gold sequined purse. Dangling from her left ear, a large, gold star earring. She has misplaced its mate, but she brushes off the fashion imbalance with wit declaring, "I'm a one-star general." Her clinic doctor said about Lady Margaret, "She has such a luxuriant word salad and flight of ideas. They are so scattered, but all of (her) oblique references to the Shriners, the Mafia and the mob and living in style are all rooted in some interesting realities."

On days where her reality was elusive, she would call the church and leave protracted, rambling and slurred demands on the telephone answering machine. Lady Margaret once was a member of the upper middle class. She lived in El Paso, Texas with her husband, son, and daughter. But in 1966, that world ended with her first hospitalization and she has never gone back. Lady Margaret has a tiny room in a rundown hotel. She lives on a government subsidy of $545 per month. She has a roof over her head, but can afford little else.

Transformation for Lady Margaret means building a relationship of trust over time. Using that trusting relationship and opening her eyes to the possibilities of managing her delusions with medication would be the first step to making a new, reality-based life for herself. This new life, lived in pathways of transformation for Lady Margaret, places a big responsibility on us, the Christian church. Lady Margaret will never achieve self sufficiency, but in community, with a local church, she has taken a significant step forward to a more safe and secure life.

In every urban area we will see the people on the street who are having a conversation with no one in particular. Julian did that. Julian would stop by the church to use the restroom, get a cup of coffee or a drink of water. Sometimes he would stop by just to get in out of the heat. Julian would chatter away in his chair. He was having a conversation with a voice inside his head. Apparently, this voice was very funny. Julian would say something and then pause for a moment, listening to that voice, and then he would laugh and laugh some more. Others would push their grocery carts filled with treasures down the street. Aluminum can collections would take some room away from basic necessities; a blanket and cardboard for sleeping. The cardboard was important as a mattress but more valuable as moisture control. Cardboard has few properties which soften sleeping on the ground but it will keep you free from cold coming through the ground and sometimes is a help with keeping away the bugs. Everything was stuffed in this rolling cart. A street wise friend asked me one day, "John, do you know what they call the grocery carts homeless folks push down the street?' "No," I answered, "What do they call the carts?" "Wire Winnebago's."

Two different times in the last six years, Julian was picked up because law enforcement believed him to be a danger to himself. Julian was taken to the state hospital, stabilized on medication, and then released back to the streets. The voices inside his head would go quiet with the medication, he said, but it never lasted long. Julian found it difficult to be compliant in taking his meds because of the side effects of fatigue, slurred speech, etc. Gradually he would stop taking his meds and the voice in his head returned, frightening to others, but funny to Julian. In the most active stage of his illness, Julian would wear a heavy coat, a jacket, and sweaters underneath. He would do this in the summertime when the temperature was 90 degrees and above! A mental health professional explained to me, "We don't know why, but bundling up is often part of the disease."

Anytime you see folks who are poor walking the streets, bundled up in hot weather, you can be certain they suffer from some form of untreated mental illness. What I did understand was passers by on the sidewalk would give wide berth to Julian. They were afraid of him, even though I knew him to be a gentle soul. Transformation for Julian means access to ongoing mental healthcare for the poor, and a church community that will meet him where he is on his path.

Transformation demands that we form an intentional partnership between local churches and federally funded mental health programs. *Our* transformation happens when we open our eyes and recognize Julian's need for love and our need to love him. We are not diagnosticians, but Julian is likely to continue his cycle in and out of reality. Our transformation is linked to our local church's ability to love and support Julian in his delusional as well as lucid moments. Like Lady Margaret, Julian needs our community to achieve modest gains in his own pathway of recovery.

Chemical Abuse

Luther's struggle was alcoholism. Luther would drink each day and all day long. Luther was bright, articulate, and likable. He has been in detox and more extended treatment programs many times. It was his revolving door. The longest time of sobriety for Luther was one year. He was in a transition house, living with other men who struggled with addictions. Luther worked while he was sober. He had a job as a computer technician for a time, bought a car, and even worked at the church. One week he was late for work two different days. The following week, Luther did not come in or call on Monday. We had seen the signs of tardiness and absenteeism many other times, and we were worried. Soon our fears were realized in reports from the street: Luther had fallen off the wagon; he was drinking again. In the world of recovery there is saying "relapse is a reality, but not a requirement." After several weeks, Luther finally showed back up at our church's doorstep; he was drunk. In a familiar and often repeated request he asked to borrow money. "You know I'm not going to give you any money Luther," I said. "We've been at this place before."

"Yeah but you can't blame a guy for taking a shot. What about a job, can you give me my job back?"

"We cannot talk about a job until you go to detox and rehab. Are your ready to go? I'll drive you over there right now."

Luther thought for a minute, actually considering it. Then he said "Naw, Doc, I'm not ready yet. I need a drink first!" Then he stumbled out the door to disappear for another week. One morning we received a phone call saying Luther was trying to break into a rent house he had once shared with a friend, and had apparently gone around to the back door. That is where the police found him. He tried to run, but he was so intoxicated that he fell down and was covered in grass clippings when the police officers handcuffed him. When I pulled up to the scene he was in the back seat of a squad car looking miserable. After I identified myself to the officer I went over to Luther and talked with him through the open window. It is impossible to reason with a drunk. So I made no attempt to do that with my friend Luther. I said, "Luther, we don't know what to do anymore. You have so many possibilities for making a new life for yourself but your throw away each opportunity that comes to you. I love you, man, but I cannot stand by and watch you kill yourself!"

He listened silently and then said, "Touch me, man; hug my head." He leaned forward and I reached through the back seat open window and I hugged his head. Then the police took him away on a charge of breaking and entering. It was the last time I would see Luther alive. He was found dead on a Saturday morning, floating face-down in a river downtown. The disease finally won. If people like Luther are to experience transformation, they will need to walk a path with others. Detoxification, residential treatment, faithful commitment to recovery meetings, and active participation inside a local church community are steps on that path. It is hard work. Many times it means two steps forward, maybe a slip, sometimes a relapse, and then back to the difficult, intentional transformation work inside a compassionate, caring community. We don't give up until God does.

Adam was not an alcoholic, he was addicted to heroin. Wanda House, an addict in recovery herself and a specialist in the church's ministry with people who have been incarcerated, addicted, or both, tells the following story about Adam:

> "I met Adam in 1996 when he was a client in the prison system. He is a 43-year-old Hispanic male and has been trying to get clean (heroin dependent) for many years. When I saw him again at the church's day center, I could not believe it! Anyway, he went back and forth getting clean and then using, getting clean and then using. I sent him to a treatment center for 90 days and he did well. He got out and hooked up with the same using girlfriend, and went back out. He continued this for a while. Each time his mother came to church begging me to help him and we would try it again.
>
> "Whenever he hit bottom, he would come to me in

tears. I sent him to another treatment center and he did well as long as he was there, but when he got out he inevitably started using again. He was arrested and told his mother not to bond him out because he wanted to get his life together. He got out on his own recognizance and I got him a job cleaning the day center. Some months back, he had stolen some gold earrings from his mother, and it was haunting him. So he went to the pawn shop and put some gold earrings in lay-away. Addicts do suffer from extreme guilt about certain things even when caught in the horrors of addiction. He was so proud about the earrings, showing me the little ticket every time he made a payment.

"Then one day when he was cleaning the center I thought I noticed a difference. The difference is always in the eyes and he was no longer laughing at silly comments. I asked him if he was using again. He said, "No," but I knew that was a lie. The next day he didn't come in, and it finally came out that he was no longer clean. Some time went by and I put an all points bulletin out on him with those on the street. He came in, cried, went to treatment again but did not stay the whole time. No sooner had he left treatment than he was arrested for stealing. His sister, who is an attorney in Dallas, called and asked for suggestions. I suggested a treatment facility *out of state*! We cannot run from drugs but often times your chances are better when you start fresh. To make a long story even longer, when he was released (from jail), we sent him to a facility in another city and he will be going to transitional housing in that town after his 30 days are finished."

Transformation for Adam will mean working his program every minute of every day. It will mean reconnecting with his mother. It will mean staying away from the girlfriend and his old community where all his friends are using. It will mean buying some gold earrings for his mom. It will mean finding another church community for support, love, hope, and accountability.

Whereas Adam is at a very basic step in his pathway of transformation, others find themselves further into their transformative life. We recognized this in Don and Wanda tells his story as well:

"Don is a 43-year-old black male who is crack cocaine dependent. He started coming to the church's day center two years ago with his wife. They would come to shower, wash clothes, to eat on Wednesdays and Sundays and every time I would see them, I would trap them. Their whole goal when coming to the church was to receive services and dodge me at the same time. An addict knows another's symptoms. He knew he couldn't con me. He would get so sick of me until he finally decided the only way to get me to back up was to become disrespectful. So Don began to be sarcastic in his answers. I let him know real quick that this tactic will not back me up.

"He was caught stealing from the church and was selling the merchandise on the streets. I told the director what I saw and we called him in. He somewhat admitted to it and we prayed for him. He was not ready for treatment. Time went by and he started volunteering in the day center. One thing led to another and he was offered a position with me as my assistant and he has been the best one I have had, including the assistants who were not addicts and not from the streets. He is still with me and I am helping with his budget. They have gotten their apartment and they are street legit (have proper ID) and starting to pay off an old loan. It reminded me that some people can do this without going to treatment. Though everyone has their biases, we must not let it interfere with our heart. Remember, nobody is hopeless!"

Hard Times

Not everyone on the streets suffers from untreated mental illness, or alcohol and drug abuse. About a third of those who find themselves homeless have had a bad run of luck. They are homeless because they are inside a particularly difficult life circumstance that could happen to any of us, but unlike most of us, they don't have a safety net. Suppose someone finds a job working and receives minimum wage. In order for one person to support himself and allow no more than 30% of their monthly wage to be spent on housing in Texas, the hourly wage must be at least $9 per hour—well above minimum wage! Even at $9 per hour, it will take a full year of uninterrupted, steady work to achieve any measure of stability. So let's just suppose that this worker got more than minimum wage and had a shot at getting life together. Then in the first 90 days, life happens. Hourly wage persons who get sick and miss a week of work will find they have lost their jobs due to illness and missed time from the job. For example: let's take the mom who works in the service industry, and let's suppose she was lucky enough to have her child enrolled in a government-funded daycare program so she is able to work. If her child catches the flu, she cannot put that child in daycare while the child is ill. By law children must be free from fever for at least 24 hours before that child can return to daycare or preschool. While many could contact friends or grandparents, she is estranged from her family and too new in the city to have a network. So Mom has to stay home and nurse the youngster back to health. That can be the end of her employment.

If the job disappears, then single parents quickly find themselves late in paying rent or utilities. Next step in the slippery slope is eviction from an apartment.

Even if the single parent and children can move in with a friend or relative, under cramped conditions, the homeless family's welcome soon runs out. Maybe they sleep in a car or an abandoned building. Hiding from case workers with Child Protective Services, this mother's worst nightmare is separation and foster care. Helplessness and hopelessness rule. The transformation pathway from poverty into stability for this mom and her family means regaining housing and employment, parenting classes, maybe schooling, and certainly the participation of a loving local church community.

Middle- and Upper-Class Addictions

We recognize that people who suffer from untreated mental

illness can walk a pathway into transformation. We know that those who struggle with the disease of alcoholism or drug abuse likewise have a pathway of transformation available once they become sick and tired of being sick and tired and there is commitment to be different. Middle and upper class church folk likewise understand that some people fall on hard times. We understand that life can rise up and knock us down. This third pathway of transformation brings hope of recovery from economic, social, or physical devastation. But we are not through naming all the pathways of transformation if we only speak of these three.

I was reminded of the fourth path of transformation by a friend and colleague in the church. He reminded me that everyone needs to be in transformation, not just those from the street. It is the cornerstone of our faith in Jesus Christ. "We're talking about pathways of transformation for those who are drug or alcohol dependent, the untreated mentally ill and people facing desperate financial situations, but what about us? What about you, me and the rest of the people in the pews? Don't we need a pathway of transformation too? "He's right. We do.

Mutual transformation happens when everyone acknowledges their own personal need to be transformed. Mutual transformation happens when we accept the truth that as human creatures, we are more alike than we are different. Mutual transformation happens when we realize that the poor have as much to give us as we have to give them. We have as much to learn from the poor as the poor have to learn from the middle class. When we are in the same space, at the same time, sharing our stories with equal air time and equal attention, mutual transformation has a chance. We can learn why our "help" often doesn't help.

Take the single mother on the streets we spoke about earlier. Many churches participate in a big hearted program designed to help families. The churches open their doors to a family for a week or even a month, allowing the family to stay in their building. The church feeds the family and interacts with them. The children are put back in school, and ideally everyone is back on the path to self sufficiency, right? Only at the end of the week or month, the family moves to a new church and the process continues, then another new church, etc. until theoretically the mother gets on her feet. This system was worked out because it was too difficult for churches to undertake the responsibility for more than a few weeks at a time, but it doesn't take much imagination to see how hard this is on the recipients of our largesse. It simply isn't what is needed. What is needed are long-term stability and accountably, the formation of a network of friends and "adopted" family, and the grounding in a community of faith that encourages and believes in transformation. What is needed for the family is to stay in one church with one group of people who work with the family to secure permanent housing and employment. For the mother to get the help she needs, we have to change.

In the world of our culture's poor and marginalized people, the language of addiction and recovery is well known.

Staying connected to God, the church, family, and friends, often involves a battle with addiction, and always involves a battle of the will. The churches that have been in ministry with the poor and marginalized tend to be independent, fundamentalist, and Pentecostal churches. These churches provide the language that speaks to people on the margins. It is the language of spiritual warfare, a raging battle between good and evil, God and the Devil, weakness and the will, the drug and maintaining sobriety. These are hard, sometimes violent testimonials with life and death consequences. They are basic and raw conversations, filled with passion and a hunger to be rescued, saved, by Jesus.

Middle class people rarely talk that way. Middle class Christians talk of sin, repentance, and forgiveness. It is a very orderly, sanitized process. Sin is when we are unkind in word or deed, repentance is when we say, "I'm sorry," and forgiveness is the expected response to anyone's "I'm sorry." There is no cosmic battle here, no spiritual warfare. We confess our sin of being impatient with our children or speaking a harsh word with a raised voice. We confess our sin of saying "damn it" out loud or failing to send a "get well" card to our colleague at work. Middle class people basically do the right things at the right times with the right people, but sometimes make mistakes (sin) that need to be straightened out (repentance) and hopefully will be excused (forgiveness).

Middle and upper class people in our local churches practice a form of socio-economic elitism. We do not know persons who find themselves in poverty and we behave as if we are superior to poor and marginalized people. Remember the Pharisee who prayed on the street corner (Matthew 6) and thanked God he, this righteous man, was not like those sinners? Our practice of elitism is not much different. We judge the persons who find themselves in poverty and if we were truly honest, we would confess our feelings of superiority because we are not poor ourselves. When we understand our "sin" to be as destructive to us spiritually as the addiction is to the street addict, we have entered into mutual transformation.

Gerald May, author of *Addiction and Grace: Love and Spirituality in the Healing of Addictions*, has written eloquently about the similarities between the theological language of sin and the disease language of addiction. He says that sin is an addiction for human beings, whatever form it takes. When we as middle and upper class peoples acknowledge and testify to our own addictions and need for God to walk with us through our own battles in recovery, then we might share community across socio-economic lines. When I led a program called "We Are All Addicted to Something" at a downtown religious leader's gathering in our city, it was difficult to get this message across. "We are all addicted to something," I said. "We just can't see it in ourselves as easily as we see it in the hard core addict on our streets." One pastor said, "I know 'all sin and fall short of the glory of God,' but I'm not sure all are addicted. I don't think I am addicted to anything." I decided to push further. "Look around this circle," I instructed. "Look at your neighbor across the table. Everyone in this room is a prominent pastor in our city. I am just guessing, but I would bet that many of us in this room are addicted to our own over-sized egos!" I feel confident that these pastors did understand what I was saying at that point, because I never again received another invitation to talk before the group.

My addiction is not cocaine, heroin, or alcohol. My addictions are to my ego, control, lots of attention, the good life filled with toys, work, and more. My spouse says she is addicted to anxiety, and we both share an addiction to food. I battle my addictions (sin) every day and my recovery (forgiveness) is directly related to naming my addiction (confession) and drawing ever closer to my God and my Savior (redemption). Once we say it out loud, in this way, we increase our ability to connect with our brothers and sisters who know addiction first-hand. Without such confessions, naming what gets in the way of our being who God calls us to be, we cannot sustain any small group or church life with those who struggle with substance abuse. Addiction is such a part of the landscape of the street, as well as the bane of the rich and affluent, that we cannot continue to remain so ineffective at addressing it. To address it effectively, we must begin by naming our common ground.

We had a Bible study at the church with 15 members who were culturally, racially, ethnically, and socio-economically diverse. It was a survey course and we were moving through the Old Testament. We were on the story of Joseph, and how he had interpreted the dream for fellow inmates in Pharaoh's jail. Joseph interpreted the Cupbearer's dream; "Within three days Pharaoh will lift up your head and restore you to your position and you will put Pharaoh's cup in his hand, just as you used to do when you were his cupbearer. But when all goes well with you, remember me and show me kindness; mention me to Pharaoh and get me out of this prison." (Genesis 40:13-14 NIT) Joseph's interpretation was true and the cupbearer was restored. Yet the cupbearer did not did not show Joseph kindness and did not help Joseph get released from prison. Two years later, Joseph was still incarcerated.

The middle and upper class members of the class were incensed. "It is unthinkable that Joseph gave such a gift to the cupbearer and received nothing in return! It is inexcusable what the cupbearer did. He had two years to speak up! He should have said something!"

Our members who were newly off the streets, most of whom had done hard prison time and many who were new to sobriety from chemical abuse and living in a transitional home, saw things differently. "You've got to understand what spending time in prison does to a man," they said. "A man has got to stay 'under the radar.' Inside prison you don't say nothin' to nobody! After he got out, that cupbearer was scared to speak up cause the system already messed him over once!" Two different worlds came together inside a Bible study that day. The result was one step taken on the pathway of mutual transformation.

God is present in the mystery of people who would never otherwise speak to one another, coming together in the name of Jesus inside a local church. A young woman reported her walk of mutual transformation, which began early with her involvement as a volunteer in the Church's Sunday morning breakfast program. She had come for her weekly experience of "drive by charity," but she left that morning receiving much more than she was able to give.

"I had been involved in planning the Café from the first, but I actually missed the first Sunday of serving because my mom had just died. I returned to town the second week of Café being opened, Easter Sunday, and was pouring syrup in a bottle. Tears just began flowing from my eyes when a homeless man asked me, 'What's wrong?' I simply told him I was sad because my mom had just died. He put his hand on my shoulder and said he was sorry. I realized, at that moment, that my sorrow did not have to be my own—but that others would share my pain and my joys. It was one of those transforming moments that completely got my attention." Real transformation happens when we realize the poor have as much to give us as we have to give them. Mutual transformation is when we are transformed together, rich and poor alike.

CHAPTER 4

FROM HANDOUT TO MINISTRY

It sounds trite but is true: If you want to move from handout to ministry, if you eschew the world of "drive by charity," if you are ready to stop "playing church" and want to "be the church," then pray about it. If you belong to a local congregation that wants to make a difference, and you wonder what God has in store for your future, then pray about it. Pray for God to direct your congregation to ministry *with*, not *to*, the poor and marginalized. Pray for God to open your eyes and the eyes of your congregation to see those who experience marginalization among you:

- immigrants
- those who suffer from mental illness
- chronic street people
- situationally homeless
- those who suffer from chemical abuse
- those who suffer from alcohol abuse

- those who have been in prison
- divorced persons
- single parents
- children who have been sexually abused
- children in special-education classes
- African Americans
- Latinos
- Arab Americans
- Muslims
- those persons confined to a wheelchair or with other disabilities
- prostitutes
- high school drop-outs
- minimum-wage earners
- those who are addicted to gambling
- Jewish Americans
- mixed-race persons
- gays, lesbians, transgendered, transsexuals
- persons who suffer from hunger
- persons who are poor
- women and men who have been physically or emotionally abused

One small town congregation took this list, added more possibilities and then got down to some serious praying, convinced that God would answer their prayers for guidance. As a result, this congregation, filled with young families, saw an assisted living home close to them and began a ministry with the residents. The elderly, who knew neglect and isolation first hand, experienced transformation through the companionship and attention of church members. The church members experienced transformation by developing a new, more diverse, congregation filled with surrogate parents and grandparents well past retirement age.

Another congregation, mainly elderly Anglo and located in a changing neighborhood, prayed for God to reveal a ministry with the marginalized of their poor neighborhood. Just the daily prayer together raised their awareness to the point that one day, a member noticed an elementary aged Latino boy and struck up a conversation. It was the child's birthday but there would be no birthday party because his family was desperately poor. This church member saw his chance encounter with that boy as answered prayer. He organized a group from the church to canvas the neighborhood and find out the birthdays of all the children who lived near the church. "We can't do much," he said, "but we know how to throw a birthday party." They began to have birthday parties during the year for all the children in their neighborhood. At those parties these older, Anglo, church members would have conversations with the Latino adults and children of the neighborhood. It took some time for things to get rolling but this is a congregation growing in diversity as a result of God's answer to prayer. They changed because they quit worrying about the wear and tear on their property, or whether or not they would be burglarized. The neighborhood changed its view of the church as being isolated from their problems and uninvolved to seeing the building and its congregants as a safe haven and community resource.

At one church we served in the center of the city, the answer to prayer for ministry with marginalized led us to see the people on the streets. We wanted a deeper connection with those in our downtown area who happened to be homeless. Our Sunday morning breakfast was doing well but we prayed for a way to go deeper in our relationships. God answered that prayer, and the *Prayer Picnic* was born.

Two men from the church prayed and decided to lead a Wednesday night prayer group. "It was something we could do and we didn't have to spend a lot of money to get it done!" they said, smiling at their own ingenuity. It was a modest beginning. One Sunday morning an announcement went out to those assembled for breakfast. "We will be meeting for prayer on Wednesday night; all are welcome to attend." The first few weeks there was a gathering of 4-6 people. That was gratifying but fell short of the leaders' goal for ministry. "How can we get more people to come?" was their question. There was a conscious decision to turn the prayer group into a prayer *picnic*. When one of the leaders began to bring sandwiches and drinks, God added to their numbers weekly. This was further reinforcement for them that ministry with the poor and marginalized is strengthened when people eat together.

Soon the group outgrew the church narthex as a meeting place. The Prayer Picnic relocated to our fellowship hall. Soon the group outgrew the ability for one leader to provide sandwiches and drinks. Other small groups within the church began to cook and serve meals from our kitchen. The prayer time expanded to a prayer and recovery time. "What is keeping you from being who God created you to be?" was a question that followed prayers of petition and intersession. All who attended the Prayer Picnic met the expectation of staying connected with what was happening in the group. No one was forced to speak, yet all were invited to share. It took time to build trust among participants. Most of the poor and marginalized attendees came with suspicion and caution. "What are these doctors and lawyers up to? What is their agenda? Why should I bare my soul here?" No one asked these questions out loud, but the expression on the face of newcomers was easy to read.

Gradually, everyone who attended—rich, poor, and middle class—came to realize that our church leaders were committed to this ministry. We were in this for the long hall. This was not just another one night stand. Trust grew. One man, who slept with the stars as his roof each night, spoke up: "I have been coming here for three months and I have never said a word. For weeks, I came only for the meal. I would sit and listen to your stories. I have taken every drug you can name. My family won't speak to me and I have been in prison most of my adult life. I am tired of this life. I am tired of living on the streets. Tonight I came depressed and ready to end it all. I need to take a chance. I am asking for your help." The members of that prayer picnic listened to him, accepted him just as he presented himself, met him at this early place in his pathway of transformation, and pledged to join him in mutual transformation, his and theirs.

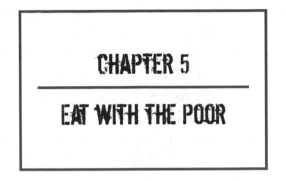

CHAPTER 5

EAT WITH THE POOR

S omeone once said, "Morality begins at 1500 calories a day." This means that we cannot expect that people are going to make sound moral decisions if they are hungry. Food and water are the most basic needs of all human beings. Shelter, clothing, companionship, and community come in a distant second to our primary need for food and water, therefore it makes sense that any ministry with poor and marginalized persons begins with food. We eat to take in the necessary calories to make it through the day. We eat together to build connections through community. We are social creatures. Eating together is necessary for survival.

The gospel of Luke talks about eating together. Zaccheus is a reviled tax collector during the time of Jesus. According to Scripture and tradition, Zaccheus climbs a sycamore tree to watch the parade led by Jesus. Jesus spots him up in the tree and goes to talk with Zaccheus saying, "Come on down Zaccheus, and I will eat with you today!" Zaccheus is so overcome that someone would offer him this basic act of intimacy, that he is changed. As a result of Jesus' invitation, Zaccheus says, "Whatever I have stolen from others, I will give back ten-fold!" Jesus says, "Salvation has come to this house today." Zaccheus is now on the pathway to transformation, all because they sat down and ate together.

On the road to Emmaus, the resurrected Jesus was an unknown stranger to his walking companions. They talked about the events of the last three days but never identified Jesus as the focus of those events. During those moments, they had no idea who he was. Jesus acquiesced to their pleas that he stay with them for the night. It was when they ate together that Jesus was made known to them.

In the Old Testament, *hesed* is a practice of welcome and hospitality among the Hebrew people. *Hesed* requires that the host and the sojourner eat together to signify welcoming and connecting with the stranger. It is clear to me that eating together is the sign of real community more than any other behavior named in the Hebrew or Christian Scriptures.

Human beings are the same now as they were then. Transformation has a chance when we eat together. My father-in-law lived with us in the last few years of his life. When we would go out of town, we worried about Jerome, who was in his 90s. As a dutiful daughter, Karen would contact friends and church members in order to line up people to stop by or call Jerome each day we were gone. Jerome never asked Karen to set these things up, he communicated to us that he could take care of himself, but he appreciated the attention from those who would look in on him during the day. A friend and church member called our house and talked with Jerome:

"Jerome, I am set to come by one day this week while Karen and John are out of town. I need to know what day is best for me to bring you lunch?"

Without hesitation, Jerome spoke up, "Whatever day you have the time to stay and eat with me."

The lesson from my father-in-law did not escape me. It was not enough to feed persons who happened to be poor. If we were to be in community and have hope for our transformation as well as the transformation of those who happen to be poor, then we have to eat together. In the early days of our Sunday morning feeding program, our church volunteers would serve food to the hungry who could not afford to buy their own meals. Many of the volunteers sensed the distance, though, which still separated us. How can we become more of a community with our brothers and sisters in poverty? How can we become one? How can we share transformation together?"

The answer was to eat together: break bread, have table conversation. One church member took the first step. He stood in line like everyone else, picked up his plate, stopped by to get syrup poured on his pancakes, spied an interesting face of a man who happened to be homeless sitting alone, and went to sit down next to that man. After a time he said, "Hi, my name is Bill," and got no response from across the table. He tried once more with the same result. Finally, as he could see his table mate was nearly finished and this opportunity would soon get away from him, the church member spoke. "Listen, I've got to be honest. I'd like to talk with you but I don't know how to strike up a conversation since our worlds are so far apart. I don't know what to say. Maybe if you would tell me your name and some of your story we could use that as a beginning. Do you have family here? Where did you stay last night? What made you come here this morning?" His efforts were rewarded. A homeless man who was used to being ignored and shunned responded positively to someone who genuinely wanted to know him. The connection was made because they first ate together.

Ministry with the poor is not just eating one meal together. It is not just having a clinic one day, one Bible study, or on one occasion, putting out coffee and water for hydration. Ministry with the poor demands that we establish trust with those who have been marginalized all their lives. The question from persons who are on society's margins is, "Are these people willing to walk the talk?" I was unexpectedly afforded the opportunity to demonstrate the church's commitment to that walk in an unexpected way.

CHAPTER 6

YOU'RE UNDER ARREST!

We had a day center in the church, initially set up as a safe place for homeless persons to hang out. Soon it became a place where people could come and get copies of identification papers, secure a job, get a shower, wash clothes, participate in recovery groups, find a job, and connect with mental and physical healthcare as needed. After our church day center had been in operation for one or two years, someone came to my office and told me in an excited voice "John, the cops just came into the day center and took someone away!" I jumped up and ran to see what had happened. The intake specialist in the day center said, "Two policemen came in, stood around looking into the day room and never said a word. I asked them, 'Can I help you?' and they said, 'We'll let you know when we need your help.'"

"I asked them again, 'Officers, may I help you?'" the specialist explained, clearly frustrated," and they simply brushed me aside, went into the day center, grabbed this guy by the arm and drug him outside."

"Where did they take him?" I asked.

"Right across the street, through the back door of the hotel" he answered.

I didn't wait to hear more. I took off across the street, opened the door and headed down a long, narrow stairway to the basement of the hotel. As I turned a corner in that basement I saw a room filled with computerized surveillance screens and four men standing inside. One man appeared to be a security guard for the hotel. Another man was the member of our day center who had been drug to this spot, while the other two men were police officers, one standing next to the homeless man while the other was watching the monitors with the security guard. Without saying a word, I went and quietly positioned myself next to my homeless brother. For a few moments the officers continued their investigation and I went unnoticed. Finally, one of the officers asked me;

"Who are you?"

"I am one of the pastors from the church next door where you came to remove this man and we need to talk!" I said.

"Sir you need to wait outside and we'll talk later," the officer responded.

"I will not wait outside and we will talk now," I demanded. "You cannot just come into God's house and take this man away!"

"Sir, I told you to wait outside!"

"Officer, no one has the right to come and take a man out of God's house!" I repeated.

"Sir, if you do not leave the premises now," the officer threatened, "I will place you under arrest."

I had a decision to make. I didn't know if the officer meant what he said or not, but I could see I was frustrating his efforts to do what he believed was his job. I did not want to risk arrest, but I was unwilling to leave my homeless brother down in that basement all alone with the security guard and those two police officers. I did not want to hinder their investigation with the video monitors but I wanted to be an observer of this event. I did not know these police officers. I did know that *some* police officers are more likely to treat poor and marginalized people with a higher level of dignity and respect if there is an outside observer present. I wanted to be that outside observer. There are too many stories of persons being mistreated while in custody. I could not take the risk of that happening in this instance so I responded:

"Go ahead and do what you have to do, but I will not leave my brother's side."

The next words I heard were, "Turn around, face the wall and spread 'em!"

Handcuffs hurt when applied behind the back by an agitated police officer, and I felt it. The officer grabbed me by the arm and transported me back up the stairway, through the door, and onto the sidewalk. Back on the street I noticed a crowd of members from our day center had gathered across the street.

"Let him go. He is our pastor," One member said.

"That's OK, this is just a misunderstanding," I explained. "Everything is going to be all right."

"What can we do, John?" someone else shouted from across the street

"Call the news media," was the first thing that came to my mind.

The arresting officer pulled me down the sidewalk and transported me just one block to the nearby bike patrol substation. I was unceremoniously dumped in a chair in the outer office. Before he went back to consult with his shift supervisor I said, "Talk to the lieutenant, he knows me, and he'll clear this whole thing up." Soon after the officer disappeared into the back room, the lieutenant did come out to talk with me.

"I didn't do anything, honest!" I pled my case, confident that my friend would make this all go away. "I just said I wouldn't leave my brother alone down in the basement with these officers. This is a big mistake."

"John, John, John," the lieutenant responded. "When my officer gives you an instruction, you have to do what he says."

"But you are his boss," I kept on. "You know my heart is in the right place, tell him this is a big misunderstanding."

"I can't do that," he replied. "If the arresting officer wants to go through with the arrest, I can't keep that from happening."

Now it was becoming real to me. I was going to jail. That was surprising to me. I never believed that would happen. It was in that moment that my spouse and co-pastor, Karen burst into the station. I found out later that one of the members of our day center had come over to get her when the police took me to the station;

"Karen, the police just hauled John off to the station," was the report.

Karen, thinking this report was made about another man named John, who was a self-professed alcoholic and frequently got into scrapes with the law, said without looking up from her desk, "I'm not surprised, I wonder what he has done this time?"

"No really, I think you should come," the reporter insisted.

"Go and find John and tell him. He is better at handling these things when day center members get in trouble with the police," she casually responded

"It's not *that* John who the police arrested, it's *pastor* John!"

When Karen came through the door, she looked at me and without hesitation, lit into the police sergeant behind the desk:

"Take those handcuffs off him this minute! Can't you see they are digging into his arm?" Then she leaned in close to my ear and whispered in obvious distress, "Sometimes you make me crazy!"

Turning her attention to the desk sergeant again she continued with her protest, taking the same tack I had tried, to no avail. It was clear that the lieutenant could not, or would not, bail me out of this tough spot. I was going to jail.

The sergeant, appointed to take me to county lockup was a nice guy. He came out and smiled, "I'm going to move your handcuffs out from behind you back unless you are dangerous."

I smiled back, "Nope, I'm not dangerous, I think I can behave myself."

I was put in a patrol car and taken down to the county jail. This sergeant told the officer riding with us in the car, "You wait here, let me go inside and tell them who we have."

Intake at the county jail is humiliating. We began with checking and bagging my belongings, and cell phone, taking my belt and my shoelaces so I wouldn't use either to harm myself, and fingerprinting. All that took nearly an hour to complete. Then I was placed in a "tank"—holding cell meant to house up to 20 men at one time. I looked for my homeless brother who had been under suspicion with the police officers but he never appeared.

There was no dignity and respect shown to any of us in jail. Sherriff's deputies barked orders and cursed us. With only one exception, a good-hearted deputy who was firm but caring in his approach, the five or six deputies who spoke to me did so with disdain and disgust for me as a person. I remembered my previous belief that anyone who was arrested surely must be guilty and deserve punishment. My views were changing.

I was handcuffed, along with eight other men and escorted before the justice of the peace. While several others were released for time served, the judge told all of them to sit down together while she read my report. After a few minutes we were told to stand up and she determined my bond to be $800.

The first question from everyone who occupies the same cell is, "What are you in for?" One young man didn't wait for me to ask, he volunteered that he was in for possession. He had a traffic violation when the officer searched his car and found a small amount of weed. He was clearly high and talkative. Others looked scary, so he came over and sat next to me. "What are you in for?" he asked me

I told him who I was and why I had been arrested.

"No, really, what are you in for?" he asked again.

"Really, it's true," I sheepishly replied.

His eyes got wide and a big smile broke over his face. "That's awesome!" he exclaimed. "It's biblical! You're in jail just like Joseph, John the Baptist, and the apostle Paul!"

"I have to admit, I never thought of it like that." I answered. "How do I get out of here?" I questioned, thinking he sounded like a veteran of these parts, and I could use some counsel.

"There is the phone where you can make a collect call. It's over in the corner. But you have to call a land line and don't bother to try the bail bondsmen listed next to the phone. They won't accept the $5 charge unless they know you as a regular customer."

I called the church. My father-in-law was working as receptionist that afternoon and he answered "Travis Park United Methodist Church." He said in a cheerful voice. A computer generated message identified my collect call like this "This is the Bexar County Jail, a collect call has been placed from our facility to this number . . . ."

I heard Jerome hang up on his end of the line.

No one had told Jerome I had been arrested, and Jerome was a product of the Depression era anyway, he was not about to accept any collect calls, much less one from the jail.

I called the church again. "This is the Bexar county Jail, a collect call has been. . . ."

"Click" went the phone on the other end while I was yelling, "Jerome! It's me, John, don't hang up!"

I called the church a third time. Mercifully, one of our support staff persons answered before Jerome could pick it up.

"Tell Karen my bond is $800 and ask if she will come to bail me out."

"I'll give her the message."

At 6:30 PM someone came in to a holding cell, 50 feet away. He saw me and shouted, "Hey, are you that preacher?"

"I am a pastor of a church downtown," I answered, thinking I must have bumped into him some Sunday morning during our feeding program. "Do I know you?"

"No, but I saw you on television just 30 minutes ago," he replied

"I wasn't on TV," I said. "I have been here since two this afternoon, I haven't talked with any news people."

"Well you're all over the evening news now, I saw you."

I went for more fingerprinting at almost 9:30. I had no idea that the authorities were, by that time, trying to extend my stay past the local ten o'clock news because pressure was mounting. In the fingerprinting process, the only words this deputy spoke were instructions to get us through this now computerized process. As we were nearing completion he asked, "Are you the preacher who was arrested?"

"Yes, I am."

"Well, you better get your thoughts together. There are TV cameras and reporters waiting outside to talk to you."

"Really?" I said, surprised and a bit scared. Sometimes TV cameras are even scarier than the police.

"Remember to tell them I took good care of you," he said.

When I was finally released, I talked to my Bishop who said, "John, it sounds like you were just taking care of the flock when you were arrested." I talked with the news media and said this was a case of only one overly aggressive police officer, and that 98% of our officers are fair and balanced. I urged everyone to pay attention to law enforcement around them and to "do your part to insure everyone is treated with dignity and respect." I then went home to rest.

The next morning, in a local restaurant for breakfast, a waitress was taking an order from Karen and me, before she left the table leaned over and said "You did the right thing." I knew then my experience was worth the grief. I had learned a lot:

- Once arrested, access to a bail bonds person from inside jail is virtually impossible. Unless some one knows some-one on the outside and that person is aware of the arrest, even if bond has been set, there is no way to get out. If I had been a stranger and poor, I would have no other option than to serve a two- to four-week sentence begin-ning the day of my arrest.

- Sherriff's deputies are underpaid and overworked.
- Handcuffs hurt when applied by an angry police officer.
- People with traffic violations are placed in the same cells as kidnappers and violent offenders
- Administrative bureaucracies, not efficiency, dominate our county jail systems.
- There is little dignity and respect for the accused in jail.
- Sometimes the report written by an arresting officer bears little resemblance to the actual event surrounding the arrest.
- I now had instant street credit because I had stood up for the rights of a homeless man in trouble with the law and spent time in jail

I now know what many middle- and upper-class people will never know. I know what it is like to spend time in jail. I know what it is like to be locked in a chain gang with seven other accused men going before a judge who will set bond. I now know what it feels like to have an angry police officer arrest me for something I did not do. I now know the indignities and disrespect of arrest and jail time. Though I would not equate the injustice of my eight-hour arrest and incarceration with the extended stays in county and state lockup endured by our homeless brothers and sisters, I now know the feeling of hard cold benches and sitting with my back against the wall because I was scared. I now know the feeling of loneliness when locked up. There was a sense that we were in a cage. We were looked on as dangerous and threatening. It was dehumanizing. Ninety percent of my homeless brothers and sisters have been arrested, and when I told them of my experience they smiled knowingly at everything I described as if to say, "Been there; done that; bought the t-shirt."

Let's be clear: I never thought I would be arrested. I might have chosen my words more carefully with the arresting officer if I had realized where our confrontation was headed. I truly thought that my buddy, the lieutenant, would make it all go away when I arrived at the police sub station. But that never happened. One more thing—I am certain the jailers knew who I was. The indignities I suffered—and they were many—were not the same as the long-term indignities a desperately poor man or woman might have to suffer. In the midst of my experience, I wondered if the correction officers saw this as an opportunity to teach me a lesson; to scare me straight. If that was the goal, it went unrealized.

CHAPTER 7

HEAR THEIR STORIES

If we want to be more than a "one night stand church" in our ministry with poor and marginalized persons then we need to begin with prayer, eat with the poor, and stand in solidarity with our brothers and sisters living in those margins. Mutual transformation is possible when we pay attention. The best way to pay attention is when we take the time to *hear their stories*.

It is not the natural inclination of middle- and upper-class folks to stop what we are doing, be still for a moment, and listen closely to the stories of people who happen to be poor. We will do that with each other, but this listening rarely extends across our socio-economic class, and almost never crosses ethnic or racial lines. We miss seeing people as flesh and blood when we fail to take time to hear their stories.

I was talking to a church leader in a coffee shop downtown in our city and a businessman overheard our conversation about ministry with the poor.

"Excuse me, I don't mean to pry, but I couldn't help but overhear some of your conversation. What organization are you with?" he asked.

"We're with the church at the corner of Travis and Navarro," I answered

"Then you are the ones who have that ministry for the homeless," he replied with recognition.

"Ministry *with* persons who happen to be homeless," I corrected him, but he had something to say and would not be slowed down by listening to others.

"I have a hard time with what you are doing. Why can't those people get a job? I see 'help wanted' signs everywhere but the homeless don't seem to want to work. I just don't understand. I'm a lawyer. We have a guy who sits out in front of our building with his guitar. He's there all day. I call him 'guitar man' because he plays the guitar and begs for money with his hat. If I wanted to help him, what could I do? What in the world can I do for him? What can I say?"

"Do you really want me to name some possibilities?" I asked him. "Is this a question you really want answered?"

"Sure I do. These are honest questions," he answered

"Then next time you see him ask him his name. He's got to have a name. Surely it would be more respectful to call him by his name than the 'guitar man' label. When you find out his name, then take some time and listen to his story. Sit down next to him on the sidewalk. It is hard to feel dignity and respect from someone who stands over you and looks down on you. Treat him like other people. Ask questions like, "Where are you from? Are you married and do you have children? What do you like to do during the day? How long have you been on the streets? What do you miss most about life before the streets? Where did you grow up?" Maybe, in hearing his name and in hearing his story, you will find you could help him with a minor city ordinance violation. Maybe you will find him interesting. Maybe you'll find the two of you have some things in common. Maybe he'll teach you something. It could happen, but you have to spend time with him and listen to his story. Take no demands or expectations to him and give your time."

"Something to think about," he mused. "But it is just not that simple." Soon afterwards, he headed back to the office and past his nameless man playing the guitar. That lawyer was wrong. It *is* that simple. We need to stop and listen to the stories all around us.

A man who happened to be homeless came to the church one Sunday morning for breakfast and a shower. While he was in line, waiting for his turn, a volunteer worker noticed his long, discouraged face.

"Tough day?" he asked

"Yeah, I finally got a job even though I'm homeless," he answered.

"Sounds like a good first step in transformation," the volunteered offered as encouragement.

"You're right," the homeless man responded with his story unfolding "but it doesn't end there. I have only had this job one week and I have already been late to work twice because I don't have a watch and don't know what time it is. I'm afraid if I'm late again I'll lose my job and I'm now just two weeks away from getting enough for a deposit for a room."

"We can fix that," our volunteer said, and took off his watch and handed it to his brother in line. "It's supposed to have an alarm in it, but I never have been able to figure out how to work the thing."

"Thank You!"

"It's OK," was our volunteer's response. "Come let me know when you put a deposit on your new place." My guess is that volunteer was like many of us. He had more than one watch. This one was not all that expensive. He was a deep disciple and took seriously the admonition of Matthew 25, "When I was hungry you fed me, when I was naked you clothed me, when I was in prison you came to visit me, and when I had no way to get to work on time, you gave me a watch." That *is* what the Scriptures say, isn't it?

Still another story spilled out on Sunday morning. We had clothes available after breakfast for those who needed to wear dark pants, black shoes, or a white shirt to work in the downtown area restaurants and hotels. It was the required uniform for almost every entry level, service industry job of the area. It was hard for supply to keep up with demand, since a large percentage of people who have the stars as their roof at night want to work. After our late worship service, someone saw a man who was homeless sitting in a corner, quietly, by himself with a black magic marker, coloring his worn out sneakers.

"What are you doing?" this church member asked him.

The man looked up for just a moment and then quickly returned to his work. "I got a job that starts this afternoon and I need black shoes. The clothes closet was out of black shoes in my size so I got this magic marker. I figure if I put on two coats that ought to be just about right!"

Many occasions I had to marvel at the creative ingenuity of poor folks. People would find themselves in desperate, last minute situations and think of ways to get by that we were unable to imagine. I can't lay claim to the numbers of shoes that my wife Karen can verify for herself, but I was sure I had five or six pairs of shoes at home including the black church shoes I was wearing. I never thought about what it would be like to try and get by with just one pair of shoes.

Joe said he looked down at the man's sock feet and thought the man had feet about the same size as his own. "What size shoes do you wear?" Joe inquired.

"Size 11."

"That's my size," Joe said, sitting down and beginning to untie the pair he was wearing. "Here, take these."

"What are you going to wear?" he asked

"I've got some more at home," Joe smiled, "but you have to give the church's magic marker back."

Joe was convinced then, as he is now, that in hearing the biblical story of Matthew intersect with this guy's struggle to keep his hospitality industry job, he had no other choice then to give my shoes away. There was more to come however, a bigger, stronger, and more powerful witness and it came from the actions of young adults and college students.

Shane Claiborne came to speak at our church and visit the Sunday morning feeding ministry. Shane is the author of *The Irresistible Revolution: Living as an Ordinary Radical*. He is a leader among college students and young adults who are ready to *be* the church and stop playing the church. After his time with us he traveled to a nearby city and spoke to a young adult gathering, about 300 in all. He told the story of what was being done in our city center with the poor and marginalized. He identified our needs and where contributions are most needed. He mentioned shoes. At the conclusion of his talk, one of the young people came forward, took off his shoes and laid them at the base of the podium where Shane spoke. Then another came and gave his shoes, then another, and still another. Young adults kept coming and piling up their shoes in that assembly hall. Two hundred fifty young adults left for home in their stocking feet that night. The organizers of that event called us and said, "Come get nearly 250 pairs of shoes!"

Never one to lose an opportunity to show the outpouring of God's love, I asked those who brought the shoes back to our church that next day to dump all 250 pair of shoes in front of our communion table for worship on Sunday. I preached a sermon that Sunday, but it wasn't necessary. All I needed to do was tell the story of this pile of shoes and my excitement at our downtown church did not just talk the talk, we were ready to walk the walk in our cotton socks.

Most of the persons who find themselves on the streets want to work. To hear their stories about trying to find and secure work reveal a lot about how our social service delivery system is broken. One man went to apply for a job as a dishwasher at a downtown restaurant. He was interviewed, and even though this employer knew the applicant was living on the street, the owner was desperate to fill the position and decided to take a chance with someone who needed another chance. This man was hired on the spot. The employer was thrilled to have someone and the man was ready to get started.

"How soon can you start?" asked the new employer

"Right away, today, now!" said the man with growing excitement.

"Great, give me your photo ID so I can complete the paperwork."

"I don't have a photo ID. I had a driver's license but it was lost or stolen some time back," explained the applicant.

"I'm sorry, son," replied the owner, "without a photo ID I can't put you to work."

"Where do I go to get a replacement driver's license?"

The Department of Public Safety should be able to help you out," was the answer. "Good luck, and as soon as you get that ID, come back. If the job is still open, it's yours."

Early the next morning our man with no identification spent his last $1.50 for a two transfer bus ride to the DPS office, took a number, and waited in line for his number to be called. When he got to the service window, the DPS worker asked,

"May I help you?"

"I hope so," our unemployed applicant replied. "I used to have a driver's license but it was lost or stolen. I don't think it expired, it is just lost and I need a replacement."

"Name on the license?" she asked, and he gave her his name. "You are correct, your license is still valid, and it will take only a minute to complete the paperwork for a replacement."

"Great!" said our guy. "This is just the help I needed."

When she had finished the paperwork she spoke again, "Now all I need is a cashier's check for $15, you can get your picture and be on your way."

"But I don't have $15," he said, "I told you my wallet was stolen!" We imagine he became angry and disrespectful at that point, seeing the impossibility of his situation. Many of the people on the street don't have a lot of social skills. They sometimes really don't know how to get the simplest things done. The same thing may be true of the clerical workers hired at many county and state offices. Maybe he was just a hustler, or maybe he took his frustration at the bureaucracy out on the DPS worker, but her frustration mounted as well.

"Why don't you go get a job then!" said the counter worker.

At the church we heard this story not once or twice, but over and over again. It was common. We found out about the need because we took time to *hear their stories*. Then we got into the Identification Recovery business. Volunteers began with an extensive interview of the person seeking a new or replacement ID. After hearing the story of personal history, these helpers came and did all the research and background work and paid for replacement photo IDs for persons on the streets. It was hard work.

People became familiar with state bureaus of vital statistics, school systems, hospitals, and any other place that would begin to establish a public record of someone's life. It was detective work combined with filling out and mailing various forms and applications. In return for the hard work of these volunteers, the recipient would do three to four hours of on-site work to cover the costs. It took about four to six weeks from the time this process was initiated until someone would receive an ID. This ministry is ongoing. It is not something that can be a one night stand.

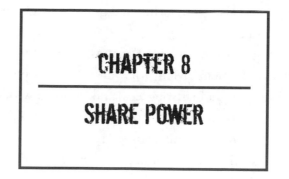

CHAPTER 8

SHARE POWER

Poor and marginalized people know the radical inequity of power in our culture. We cannot change everything overnight, but middle-class and rich folks must do their best to equalize power in relationships. This takes time and we, who are privileged, must take the initiative in bringing equality to our relationships with the poor.

We had a 501c3 charter for the feeding program and all the other ministries that were spawned from that program. We built a relationship with an independent drug, alcohol, and prison recovery personality who was a leader in a different culture. He was African American, poor, had dropped out of school after junior high school, and had been in prison three times with felony convictions. He received his ministry training inside prison and had a theologically conservative, non-denominational, pastor-centered church model. His ministry was in recovery from drugs and alcohol, and he operated a halfway house for addicts. He raised money for ministry by going from one place to another, begging for funds, and living hand to mouth.

Our congregation was, for the most part, white and middle class and affluent. Many of our elected congregational leaders have post graduate degrees, and "a brush with the law" meant no more than the occasional traffic ticket. Our pastors trained at accredited seminaries and we had a theologically progressive or liberal, mainline, consensus building church model. Our congregation had a prepared budget, following the calendar year, underwritten by pledges from an annual finance campaign.

I suggested he come before our decision -making body with his request to be taken under our congregation's 501c3 charter as a nonprofit. This was for the purpose of securing funding and support for his "House of Hope" from outside grants and agencies. I thought this was the easiest and best way for us to be partners. I was misguided.

Let's review the overwhelming messages of inequality;

- We have money and you don't. Please come before our "all white" board with your hand extended and we will decide if you are worthy to receive from our generosity.

- We have formal education and you do not. We understand 501c3 status and the paperwork necessary to maintain that designation and we will allow you to be a part of us since it is confusing to you.

- We meet around a conference table, using big words in our deliberations to determine if taking a financially stressed ministry like yours in is a prudent use of our resources.

- We would see each other socially, outside of the church, but none of us have invited you to share with us socially.

Everyone in the room had a love for Jesus Christ and a love for ministry *to* the poor and marginalized, but our mutual transformation was dependent on seeing ministry *with* poor and marginalized persons, and we were not there yet. In order to *be* different, we must *do* some things differently. Since we, the middle and upper classes are the ones who wield power in our mainline churches, we are the ones that need to change our behaviors for poor and marginalized people to feel comfortable and share community with us. The powerless are unable to grab our power; we need to give the power away. We need to step out of our middle- and upper-class comfort zones to make connections across socio-economic lines.

In our governance bodies, we need to have equal representation between persons who are poor and the middle or upper classes.

- We need our decisions to be worded in language that is easy to read for those who read at less than a high school level.
- We need to socialize together—have celebrations and parties together.
- We need to meet together in less formal settings.
- We need to have poor and marginalized disciples lead at least half of our devotionals, meditations, and public prayers in our gatherings.
- We need to dress less formally and more casually.

- We need to be inclusive of both conservative and progressive theological perspectives.
- We need to live out our faith more through our hearts and less in heads.
- We need to always search for ways to build trust with persons who happen to be poor.

The most success we had in building shared power was with our neighborhood council. As I mentioned before, our city voted in some ordinances that we felt criminalized homelessness. Since people had to sleep, and people who suffered from alcohol or drug addiction or untreated mental illness were homeless with no indoor sleeping possibilities, then our congregation wrestled with the question, "What should we do?" The question was rephrased in a way one might expect any groups of Christian disciples might ask: "What would Jesus do?" We were not handing out bracelets that night—we were in a deep dilemma.

The congregation came to a decision. Since the city did not provide the option most needed, an outdoor sleeping area, we decided to designate the outdoor space, owned by the church, as a "safe sleeping area" for persons who needed a place to rest. It is a downtown church so there is very little outdoor space, but in our flowerbeds there appeared 20-30 people each night. We were committed to maintaining this safe sleeping area until a reasonable alternative was offered by the city. With no alternative available at the start of this experiment we settled in for the long haul. Nearby businesses, restaurants, and hotels were upset.

"That's good," I said when someone reported how the hotels were bothered by an all night sleepover outside of our church. "When tax paying, powerful business men and women are raising hell with the city to do something, that works in favor for a positive resolution!"

Soon, we learned that our business neighbors were not the only problem. Those who regularly slept around our church were vulnerable, and it wasn't safe at night. We tried to find volunteers who would patrol the area throughout the night but that was difficult to do. We researched how much money it would take to have a security guard, and the price tag was out of our reach. I finally decided to call representatives of our outdoor sleepers together and asked those present, "What do you suggest we do?"

The answer came quickly, "Those of us who sleep around the church are a community. We have to watch out for each other on the streets because it is so dangerous to live like we live. We will form a 'neighborhood watch' around the perimeter of this church. We will take shifts through the night. We will watch each other's back."

"Sounds like a good solution," I replied. "Let's get some more leaders to join you and me in order to establish some boundaries of acceptable behavior agreed to by everyone who beds down here at night." The poor and homeless need to know their own gifts as much as we do, and they need the validation of their own life experiences.

So it happened, the neighborhood watch organization was born and monitored their neighborhood effectively and cleanly. We did provide some training for the neighborhood watch leaders and eventually there was a security person on site during the most vulnerable hours at night, but it was essentially self-rule. The powerless were given power and exercised it judiciously and with wisdom from the streets. After several months, the city caved in to pressure from the business community and designated some off-site locations for outdoor sleeping, even providing toilets and security personnel at these new sites.

On a related note, a new municipal court judge came on the scene that had a heart for the poor. She and I talked. She said she would not treat any of these ordinance violations as a criminal offense. She explained that if someone received a ticket for camping outdoors, blocking the sidewalk, or relieving themselves in public late at night, she would put pressure on them to get appropriate treatment in a recovery program or with a mental health worker. We had both available at our church, and she promised to designate our church as one of their community service locations for these offenders. I was thrilled.

"That's just what we want," I told her. "We are all about transformation." I convened the Neighborhood Council for yet another discussion. It was decided that if sleeping outdoors would no longer be treated as a crime, then we did not need to have a designated "safe sleeping zone" around the church any longer. The judge had spoken. No one would be required to spend any time in jail if they would just agree to take steps toward getting their lives back in order. The ruling body of our local church agreed. There was no reason to battle the ordinances any longer because the judicial system had turned toward transformation for human beings and away from criminalization of persons who happened to be homeless.

CHAPTER 9

BE WISE AS A SERPENT AND GENTLE AS A DOVE

Manipulation is a survival skill for the poor and marginalized. Persons who happen to be poor are better at manipulation than we are. Our local, downtown church never gave out money—no exceptions. There is no way for persons who have lived in the middle and upper classes all their lives to properly discern what is legitimate need as opposed to what might be a clever con. Many in the church, because their hearts are in the right place, have handed out small sums of money out of Christian compassion and, without even realizing it, have made a bad situation worse. I have spent several years in ministry with the poor and marginalized, and still I get conned.

It was the Christmas season and one of our guys from the street who was a regular volunteer in the day center announced to me that he had been sober for one month! I applauded him for working hard in sobriety and offered encouragement to stay the course. As Christmas drew closer I bumped into him again while he was doing some clean up duties in his volunteer work in our day center. His face was long and sadness was in his eyes. I asked him, "What's wrong?"

"Nothing," he said without looking up. "It is just something I have to live with."

I wouldn't let it go. "When I ask you 'what's wrong?' I really want to know."

"Nobody can really help," he said with a sigh, "but if you want to know, here it is; my daughter and I haven't spoken for five years. Since I made a mess of my life she has every right to be mad. Last night I called her and told her I was sober and this time it was different. This time I was working with a church and I knew I could make it. She invited me to come by her house and meet my three-year-old granddaughter, whom I have never seen. I told her I would come, but today I realized I can't go empty handed. I want to take a present to my granddaughter but I don't have any money."

"Wait here," I instructed. "I'll be back in a minute."

I went into our church's nursery and looked around for a toy, any duplicate toy that was age appropriate for a three-year-old little girl. I said to myself, "If I find something, I'll give it to him and replace it in the next couple of days. Then everyone wins." I came up empty, so found myself in tough spot. I wanted so bad to fix it for my new friend. I wanted his daughter to be proud of him for his month's worth of sobriety, and for his granddaughter to receive a new toy along with love from this new grandfather. At some level, I got sucked in because I rarely got to see my own daughter and granddaughter, and though I was unable to change that for myself I wanted to fix the problem for him. I couldn't go shopping with him for a toy that day, and since Christmas was closing in fast, something had to be done quickly. If a gift was to be purchased for his granddaughter, my friend ought to be the one who chose which gift it should be.

If he makes the choice, I thought, then that choice keeps some power in his hands and helps in our relationship of mutual dignity and respect. I had ten bucks in my wallet, and, after all, it was Christmas. The voice in my head rang out, *"Do not give out money under any circumstances!!"* But what choice did I have? Certainly this is a unique circumstance, with a man who has made the right choices for the last 30 days. He needed some encouragement. He needed someone to believe in him. In addition, I was estranged from one of my own daughters and she had a baby, a new grandchild of mine, whom I had seen only once. I felt my own guilt about not being a good grandfather. My "knee-jerk liberalism," which maintains that the poor are victims and never catch a break through no fault of their own, was taking over and I gave into the internal pressure.

I took the ten dollars out of my wallet, handed it to him and said, "Here, I never do this because in just about every case it is a bad idea to give money. This is to buy your granddaughter a Christmas present. Don't tell anyone you got money from me. Go, buy a present and use the rest for a bus ticket to your daughter's home. Reconnect with your family. Merry Christmas!" He thanked me, and headed out the door. I felt great.

I didn't see him again until after the New Year. As soon as I saw him I asked how his daughter had received him and how his granddaughter liked her present. He shook his head and replied, "I'm not going to lie to you. I never got to my daughter's house and my granddaughter never got her present. I took the money, went out, and got drunk. I'm sorry."

"That's great!" I said, admittedly trying to hide my disappointment but trying to look on the bright side.

"How can you say that?" he asked

"You didn't lie to me and that is a good start." I continued, "Transformation takes time. There are many starts and stops. Two steps forward and one step back is the norm, not the exception in transformation. You have a long way to go, but a huge first step is to trust me, and trust this church enough to tell us the truth. Thank you for telling me the truth!" He looked reassured and perplexed all in the same moment and it was a step forward in our mutual transformation. He began to trust me and the church more than he ever thought possible. And I learned, and re-learned, the following lessons:

- Never give money.
- Never work harder to fix someone else's problems than that person is working to fix their own problem.
- One month's sobriety is not a long time.
- I am not easily manipulated, but if someone pushes the right buttons in me, it can happen.
- We both need God's grace—him for his untreated addic-

tion to alcohol and me for my untreated addiction to fixing other people.

These lessons confirmed for me how important it is for local churches to provide work for those who have nothing. At our downtown local church we would receive four to five requests for assistance every week. The requests were primarily for bus tickets, help with rent or utility bills, medicines, and food. We were able to provide some medicines through our medical clinic. We were also able to provide food through our feeding program or other feeding programs around the city. It is true that, with all the feeding programs in our major metropolitan areas, no one needs to go hungry. With the proper information, and the chronically homeless have that information in every city, persons who are hungry can and will find food.

Our church served breakfast on Sunday, and lunch Monday-Friday. The Baptists served lunch cooked by Miss Angie. The Presbyterians served lunch one Sunday a month. The Episcopalians served lunch through the season of lent. The Salvation Army served meals each day. St. Vincent de Paul served breakfast, lunch, and dinner 365 days per year. Suburban churches would have feedings under the freeway bridge, and we partnered with a Roman Catholic Church to distribute food through the Mobile Loaves and Fishes program every evening. In our city, as in others, no one should go hungry.

Still, what about bus tickets, rent assistance, and utility bills? If we were not going to give money, then how would some people get help? It was simple; we created a way for people to work. Early on, conversations went like this:

"I need $15 for a bus pass this month so I can get back and forth to work," one guy would say.

"We don't do money," I would explain. "We do food, medical care, dental care, vision care, recovery groups, job training, clothing for work, showers, and a bunch of other things, just not money."

"How in the world am I supposed to get back and forth to work then?" protested the inquirer using the "Once again, I am a victim, hopelessly trapped in yet another unresponsive system" line of thinking.

"I have an idea," I offered. "We have some three-hour jobs we need done around the church. If you are willing to work for three hours doing some light cleaning and maintenance, we will pay you $15 in cash for those three hours." Some folks would leave without further conversation. The "nays sayers" are correct. Some people, a small percentage of folks, who are chronically poor, and find themselves on the streets, are not interested in working and not ready to take transformation steps.

Yet the vast majority of persons trapped in poverty want to work. Work provides dignity and respect for those who rarely receive it. Honest work gives a sense of pride.

"I don't want a handout man, I'm willing to work!" became a mantra for many who came through our doors.

If a church builds a work program, that church will run out of funding for the program before they run out of willing workers on Monday morning. We received so many requests for these three-hour job spots that we instituted a lottery system, a drawing on Monday of each week for the opportunity to work three hours on that Tuesday. Many a Monday morning, I would arrive at church and see 35-40 men and women waiting to draw a number, and hoping to be one of three persons who would receive a $15, three-hour job that next day.

We went from three custodians down to two and used the savings to put people from the streets to work. We used six to eight workers every week. Still the need was overwhelming. Some people were helped when our church members who employed folks in construction, landscaping, and ranching work hired some our most dependable and hard working folks from our three-hour work program. We developed a relationship with temporary labor pool companies who regularly used our day center members for day labor.

"Day labor is a crapshoot," one friend told me. "You don't know your employer and I have been shortchanged on my pay many times with those guys. Sometimes they would bail and I wouldn't get paid at all."

"How much per hour do you earn with day labor jobs?" I asked

"Minimum wage, and they take out money for transportation and your lunch when you eat. It's not enough to get a room or food for the night. You can't get ahead!"

This haunted me, I prayed about it and we began to dream new dreams and see new visions for the church. During the Katrina hurricane disaster, our church decided to bid on work in temporary shelters for the duration of the crisis, but we met with heavy resistance. The day labor companies threatened to never again use day center members after the New Orleans relocation crisis ended if we became independent contractors working directly with FEMA and not through them. We backed off. I later regretted this decision.

Day labor companies are paid between $12-$18 per hour for their day laborers. These companies then pay the worker, $6-$7 per hour. The only other costs incurred for their operation are insurance and administration. Since our church could have gotten the insurance and administration covered for about $5 per hour, per worker, we could have operated a non profit, temporary labor company and paid a living wage of $10 per hour. If a church did this nonprofit work, that church would have the opportunity to build relationships with the worker, speaking with them on a daily basis, and supporting them through their transformation towards stable lives. The volunteer and paid administrators in this church nonprofit would themselves experience transformation through this connecting, relationship building, community strengthening, and daily contact with poor and marginalized persons. This ministry would be ongoing, and not just a one night stand.

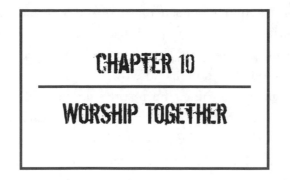

CHAPTER 10

WORSHIP TOGETHER

Middle- and upper-class folks are separated from the poor at 11 o'clock every Sunday. Not only is the 11 o'clock hour on Sunday morning the most segregated hour of any week by race and ethnicity, it is the most segregated hour by socio-economic status as well. If we want diversity in worship, we must be open to change.

Begin by viewing worship through the eyes of poor and uneducated people. How do people dress in your church? Are all the men in suits and ties? Are all the women in dresses? Who is wearing a t-shirt? Who is wearing sandals? Look around, how many people look different than you?

On Good Friday we had a liturgical tradition. At the end of the Good Friday worship service we would strip the church. We would remove all of the candles, the communion table cloth, the cross, offering plates, flower stands, and even the pulpit. We would drape black cloth over anything we found impossible to move out of this space. After we were finished stripping the church, our sanctuary looked bare and barren. In concert with the events of Good Friday, there was no life left. It was dead space because Jesus had died on the cross and the dream of God's kingdom had died with him.

On Sunday morning, the resurrection would come! We would process into the worship area in celebration of the resurrection carrying all the symbols that had been removed 2 days before. Along with another staff person at the church, I recruited some of our brothers and sisters from the streets to join the processional. Andy, a poet from the streets, dressed in a t-shirt and shorts carried in the altar paraments. With solemnity, dignity, and respect, he draped them over the table with the assistance of Detroit, an African American street hustler who wore his hair in a Mohawk cut and was chemically dependent. Barbara, who slept in our church office doorway each night, carried the collection plates. George, the shoe shine guy, with black polish visible under his nails, brought in the candles; and four huge fellows from our transitional house for parolees and crack addicts carried in our pulpit, setting it in place. The last man in was Ron. Ron was 40 years old, had green hair in a spike, visible tattoos all over his arms and neck, and was wearing earrings as well as a nose ring. Ron carried the empty cross, marching triumphant and proud, placing it carefully in the middle of our table.

One clergyperson attending worship that day said to me afterward, "That was the best Easter ever! The highlight or worship for me was the processional. It was wonderful to see all the diverse people of God in one worship service together."

At our downtown mainline protestant church, we were quick to say "Paupers and princes are in the same breadline here."

We kept a traditional worship service at 9 AM. It was a service that was highly dependent on printed liturgy. We had a choir, which sang classic church anthems with periodic ethnic and African music mixed in. Our pipe organ was featured with hymns sung from our hymnals, which were published in the early 1970s. This service rarely reached beyond the tastes and preferences of middle- and upper-class white folks. It did, however, meet the traditional worship needs of some in our local church who were pleased with the church's vision of ministry with the homeless but were not ready to change their classic worship forms. Pastors wore robes and we served communion every Sunday.

But, as advertised, we warned people to "Get ready to rock and roll" at the 11 AM service. First, we dressed down. Middle- and upper-class pew sitters came in polo shirts and slacks. Some would wear jeans. Women wore pants and a blouse. We eschewed formal attire in the name of hospitality. We did not want anyone to believe they needed "church clothes" to fit in with our 11 AM service. Second, we did a careful study of our printed liturgy. We learned our liturgy was written for a congregation that read at the college level. Our written liturgy and some of our spoken liturgy was filled with "church words." You know, prayers like;

"Lord, you are our creator and sustainer. We find sustenance through your bounty. We find solace in your sanctuary. We are empowered through the knowledge that you are omnipresent and omniscient. The restorative nature of your grace brings us to a new level of discipleship . . . ." You get the picture. We had to change.

Our written liturgy was not "dumbed down," as some critics are quick to say, but it was made more accessible with prayers like, "God, we need you. We are hurting. We are hungry for your presence. You have promised you will keep us safe. Please don't forget us." One worship service we stopped using printed liturgy altogether. Whereas many poor and marginalized people are very bright, it takes intelligence to survive hand to mouth many poor folks may not have much formal education. Many may have difficulty reading at a high school or a junior high school level. In worship we might use a call-response liturgy not printed on paper but projected on a screen. When the mix of folks who are poor and middle- and upper-class folks grew, we had more "Amen" responses. We began to have more hand raising from people who were accustomed to physically reaching up in the air to praise their God and savior.

Different things began to happen in our preaching as well. There were often surprises. One morning, Russell, one of our chronically homeless guys, came down to the front of our sanctuary while I was preaching. He walked up to me in the middle of the sermon and said, "John, I need to talk with you." Knowing that Russell was a gentle soul who had taken more drugs in his lifetime than Walgreens had on their shelves, and, as a consequence of his drug use, had fried the brain cells that would otherwise have helped him maintain boundaries, I told him "Russell, why don't you sit down in the front pew, next to Sam, and after I get through talking, we'll visit and take care of this problem together." Russell thought that was reasonable and sat down next to Sam, a psychologist and longtime member of our church who supported our local church vision and knew Russell's special needs. I finished leading worship, found Russell, and we talked through his concern.

Another Sunday morning, when I was preaching on a hot button topic, one of our guests who had just finished breakfast in our fellowship hall before worship stood up in his pew and began to openly challenge what I was saying. Leaving my place behind the podium I walked toward the man and began a dialogue.

"Brother, I want to hear your objections but please let me finish these thoughts."

"You are wrong in what you are saying and God condemns you!" he responded. I saw some very anxious ushers heading towards this man but I waved them off.

"Please, brother, I want to honor your voice, but I can't do that until our worship service has concluded."

"Forget about it!" he said. "I'll never come back here again!" Then he stormed out. I could have gone back to my sermon notes and plowed through without recognizing what had just happened with the congregation but I chose to shift the worship experience to acknowledge what had just happened. I said some things about strong differences among strong Christians. I talked about unity in the face of diversity, and honoring the passionate concerns of others as the example of giving everyone a full measure of dignity and respect. As is so often the case for worshippers, the pew sitters of that day did not remember so much what was said that morning as what we did that morning. It was an anxious time but a time worth the risk when our goal was true economic, racial, and ethnic diversity.

My favorite was Jon. Jon was an African American man who had lived on the street for years. He was very intelligent, had a photographic memory, and a passion for the worship of God. Every Sunday morning at 11 AM, he took his seat in one of the front pews with his tambourine. When the celebration band began to play, John would get carried away in the music. He would beat on his tambourine and, as the spirit often moved him, he would begin dancing. When the spirit would light on him in an overpowering way, he would carry his dancing through the isles of the sanctuary. Some in the congregation would maintain their reluctance for movement in the face of Jon's dancing but children and others who worship from the heart would join in. Jon reminded us all that worship must engage the heart as much as the brain. Jon also reminded us of the time honored Christian practice of praising God through dance.

For those of us who worshiped in the Anglo mainline protestant traditions, we had to change our thinking. In these traditions, the above mentioned worship experiences would be called "disruptions." Now, in the midst of our desire for diversity and our commitment to ministry and worship with poor and marginalized people, that which used to be a disruption is now simply a surprise. We expect surprises in worship now. Surprises are not an intrusion but an expected part of every Sunday worship flow.

A big surprise for worship came through our day center. Without anyone informing our worship team, a day center choir was formed. Our drop-in day center was filled with poor and marginalized people, some homeless and some not, who wanted to be a part of worship during the Christmas season. Someone got the idea of forming a choir that would be able to sing in worship. Everyone who wanted to participate was encouraged to come to practice. After some rehearsal time, the choir was ready to lead Christmas carols in Sunday morning.

These new choir members lined up on our risers and did not hold back. They sang loud and with a passion for Jesus. A few actually had decent pitch. Stoles draped around the neckline of the choir robes were worn backward and forward. No one cared much about fashion as their voices were lifted up in praise. While I watched and joined in the singing when instructed, I took note of the unusual scene on our chancel area. Few of these members had ever attended church before this choir performance, but now they were a part of the music program at our local church. This was more than just one night of singing carols. This was more than a one night stand; it was a commitment to build community where isolation and separation used to reign.

CHAPTER 11

THINK INDIGENOUSLY; USE AGGRESSIVE PURSUIT

For these changes to occur, for dignity and respect to be known in our community of faith, we cannot rely on invitation alone. We have to do more than invite. We must aggressively pursue persons who are poor and live on the margins.

We must give up on the notion that poor and marginalized people will come to our churches through invitation only, even a personal one. That was hard for me to understand until I learned from a lay person who knew her stuff. She had lived on the streets in the past and now worked in recovery. She was an active member of her local church. She confessed she wanted nothing to do with the hypocrisy of organized religion and found it easy to stay away. "People would invite me to church but I found it easy to fight off their religious advances." Yet now, she witnesses to the fact that she would likely be dead had it not been for the love of her local church.

In the early years of our ministry to the marginalized I was a whiney baby about my ineffectiveness in getting poor folks to visit worship. "I never fail to invite folks who eat breakfast with us on Sunday morning to come to our celebration worship service," I moaned to her, "but very few take me up on it."

"What do you say to them when you are trying to get them to come?" she asked

"I say, 'We're having worship at 11 this morning. I'd love for you to come.'" I was very proud of my invitation. I continued, "I don't say 'Please come to worship this morning if you're not too busy, or if you don't have other plans.' That is only half-hearted, and people won't come to worship services with only half-hearted invitations."

"That's not going to work," my new consultant answered. "It is hard for people who are poor to believe you really want them in worship. This is a middle- and upper-class church. If you want to have an economically diverse worshiping community, you need to aggressively pursue poor and marginalized people." She was very matter of fact and she was not finished with her instruction: "Watch closely; this is how it is done."

Stepping up to one of our regulars at Sunday morning I watched her model aggressive pursuit for me "Good morning, brother, what is your name?"

"Hank," he replied, caught off guard and suspicious of the attention

"Hank, are you enjoying your breakfast?"

"Yeah, I like it all right," he responded, beginning to relax a bit.

She pressed forward. "See that man standing over there? That is the pastor of this church."

"I know," he said, recognizing me. "That's pastor John."

"Well that man needs you to come to worship this morning. I don't know if you need to come to worship or not, but I know this man and this church need you to come to worship this morning. They need you to worship with them in order to be all God has called them to be. They can't be all God has called them to be without you." She rested for just a moment and then worked hard to close the sale, "Will you come and sit with me in worship this morning?"

Startled, but feeling a rare measure of dignity and respect coming his way he stammered through a response, "Yeah, I mean, yes, I guess I will."

"There," she said as she brushed past me, on her way to more conversations with others who were finishing their meals. "That's all there is to it!"

If we want our churches to be socio-economically diverse, we have to work hard to gain the trust of the poor. We have to share power. We have to treat everyone with a high level of dignity and respect and we must practice aggressive pursuit. It is a lot of hard work. We have to break down barriers of mistrust. We have to see things with the eyes of persons who happen to be poor and ask the questions, "What keeps me from feeling comfortable here? Why do I feel so left out and unwelcome? What could the people of this church do to help someone who is poor, like me, feel like a member of this community?"

Look closely at your Sunday morning Christian Education program. What material is being used in the adult classes? Is this material accessible to folks who have an eighth-grade or lower reading level? Does the class discussion honor everyone's opinion and distribute respect to all who are present? Are the social activities inclusive of everyone? If someone who is poor is willing to host a class gathering, will they be encouraged to do so? If the teaching role is shared by the class members and someone who is poor would like to teach are they given the opportunity?

Find out what the barriers are to their attendance for worship as well as Sunday School. For some it might be the lack of transportation. Churches have long placed "We are easy to find" maps on their websites. Along with the church address, there are driving instructions from various locations in their cities and towns. I have never seen however, instructions on how to reach the local church by bus or other forms of mass transit. To include such information, complete with where and when to catch the bus on a church website, would be a symbol of welcome to poor and marginalized people who use public transportation every day.

Welcoming the poor is our beginning. Building community with the poor is our goal. We have looked at several ways this can be accomplished by congregations determined to be economically diverse. It takes intentionality. This will not happen through simple invitation and encouragement. It will happen when our churches re-set the existing local church vision to live out the vision of Jesus Christ. Living out the gospel of inclusiveness is hard work, and will bring us into contact with interesting, engaging, smart, and funny people. Commitment to this ministry will give us wonderful stories of courageous people just trying to stay alive. They hang on to their dignity and self respect and never lose their sense of irony about the way our world works.

This story told by Fred Karnas Jr, a local church layperson in Phoenix and friend to the poor in Arizona illustrates how the personality of one man breaks through even as he is living in desperate circumstances.

It was just before Christmas 20 years ago and a group of homeless advocates had organized a candlelight march through downtown Phoenix to highlight the loss of so many of the cheap hotels that provided affordable, if not particularly safe and sanitary housing for mostly single young men. No one was arguing that the hotels should be saved, but that if we were going to remove them, we needed to build something comparable so folks with very little money could have a roof over their heads.

The march ended at Civic plaza, and as the event ended, many people stood around taking in the pre-Christmas sights and sounds and talking with fellow marchers. It was there that my friend Dennis looked across the plaza and saw a homeless man who had participated in the march. The man had used a shopping cart as a walker so he could participate. There he stood, with his crutches leaning in the cart's basket.

As Dennis watched the homeless man reached into his pocket and pulled out a hot dog, and using his candle as a miniature grill, he roasted the hot dog—one piece at a time.

As Dennis continued to watch, the man roasted a piece of the hot dog and bit it off, and then roasted the next inch or so of the hotdog.

Just after he had completed about half the hotdog, he noticed that my friend Dennis was watching him. He slowly roasted one more piece, but as he raised it to his mouth, the man looked across at Dennis and said, "Excuse me sir. Do you have any grey poupon?"

Are you open to being in community with the poor without rescuing them or judging them? The answer to this question from our local churches will give us a feel for how friendly we are towards the poor. To actively embody a socio-economic inclusivity in our local churches means a long-term commitment from the membership. It means we must resist the temptation to give up on an inclusive experiment inside the church simply because we have discovered a hiccup or have encountered resistance. We must be in it for the long haul; after all, this is not just a one night stand.

EPILOGUE

We know that churches struggle with change, yet we were surprised at the level of opposition to this ministry with the poor. Even church leaders well versed in Scripture had difficulty practicing Jesus' teachings inside our four walls. There were frequent grumblings of, "Must we have these homeless people here on Sunday mornings?" In the initial stages, some in the congregation wanted these ministries to be weekday ministries, anytime but Sunday mornings and anywhere but on our own property.

The same is likely true about any church built around mainstream America. In our stratified society, the middle and upper classes in our country are the ones who have set the boundaries placing the marginalized where they are! Still, the responses and opposition may surprise you. In reality, many congregations are entrenched in dysfunction, resistant to change, and mired in conflict. Members substitute attending meetings for the work of ministry, and preoccupy themselves with issues that don't matter to the rest of the congregation.

Many congregations feel paralyzed by a lack of money and people, and many pastors wonder what this all has to do with their original call. If you hunger for a different culture in your congregation, here are some suggested first steps:

1. If your congregation is unhealthy, deal with the sickness. No significant change can happen until the pastor and leaders recognize the need for change, and agree to pattern their life together according to the teachings of Christ.

2. Ground yourself in Scripture. Jesus was all about being in community with the marginalized of his day. Women, tax collectors, prostitutes, those suffering from mental illness, the mixed-race Samaritans, Roman goverment officials, and the poor—just to name a few—were all marginalized. Texts that will help your church in self definition are:

    - Jesus with Mary and Martha in the home of Lazarus
    - Jesus with Zacchaeus
    - Jesus with the woman who annointed his feet with oil
    - Jesus with the demoniac
    - Jesus with the Samaritan woman at the well
    - Jesus with the woman caught in adultery
    - Jesus with the Roman official
    - Jesus with the widow and the two copper coins

3. Identify people within a three-mile radius of your church who are marginalized by the community and not being

reached by the church. Involve others in the process, including those outside the church in this community assessment. To figure out what the people in your target group need, not just what you want to do for them, you must form relationships. When they trust you, they will tell you what they need.

4. From the beginning, plan for the target group to worship with and be a part of the church. Without this, you're just a social service agency. Find out what the predominant faith tradition is of those you are trying to reach (mainline, Pentecostal, Catholic, non-denominational, none) and what kind of public worship, prayer, and educational experiences that interest them.

5. If needed, make changes in worship that will bring in the people with whom you want to be in ministry. Obviously, you have to lay the groundwork to do this and bring the existing congregation along with you. The early church spread by adapting Christianity to the people they were trying to reach. Missionary work is still done this way today, and the biggest mission field is in our own backyard. Forget about homogeneity; be ready to embrace diversity, for this is the true reflection of the church in Acts.

Finally, remember we are all profoundly uncomfortable around great poverty and desperate need; this is a part of our own spiritual lives in need of transformation. A strong vision of the future of this ministry will take root inside your congregation, for this is both the promise and witness of the gospel.

Prepare your leaders for the conversations that will need to take place throughout the church that enable you to survive and thrive. Teach and practice patience in the face of resistance, and the power of the gospel will change hearts and minds. The church members who stayed, and those who came after our downtown church's ministry began, did so because they believed this ministry embodied the basic teachings of Jesus in a way they had never experienced.

Along with many others in the emergent church movement, we believe in Jesus' proclamation that the kingdom of God is at hand. We don't need to wait for empowerment; we already have everything we need to build a community of faith that embodies the gospel, and the world has never needed its transforming power more than it does now.